THE ENIGMA OF PERSONALITY

JOURNEY THROUGH THE MIND AND BODY

Other Publications:

WEIGHT WATCHERS® SMART CHOICE RECIPE COLLECTION
TRUE CRIME
THE AMERICAN INDIANS
THE ART OF WOODWORKING
LOST CIVILIZATIONS
ECHOES OF GLORY
THE NEW FACE OF WAR
HOW THINGS WORK
WINGS OF WAR
CREATIVE EVERYDAY COOKING
COLLECTOR'S LIBRARY OF THE UNKNOWN
CLASSICS OF WORLD WAR II
TIME-LIFE LIBRARY OF CURIOUS AND UNUSUAL FACTS
AMERICAN COUNTRY
VOYAGE THROUGH THE UNIVERSE
THE THIRD REICH
THE TIME-LIFE GARDENER'S GUIDE
MYSTERIES OF THE UNKNOWN
TIME FRAME
FIX IT YOURSELF
FITNESS, HEALTH & NUTRITION
SUCCESSFUL PARENTING
HEALTHY HOME COOKING
UNDERSTANDING COMPUTERS
LIBRARY OF NATIONS
THE ENCHANTED WORLD
THE KODAK LIBRARY OF CREATIVE PHOTOGRAPHY
GREAT MEALS IN MINUTES
THE CIVIL WAR
PLANET EARTH
COLLECTOR'S LIBRARY OF THE CIVIL WAR
THE EPIC OF FLIGHT
THE GOOD COOK
WORLD WAR II
HOME REPAIR AND IMPROVEMENT
THE OLD WEST

For information on and a full description of any of the Time-Life Books series listed above, please call 1-800-621-7026 or write:
Reader Information
Time-Life Customer Service
P.O. Box C-32068
Richmond, Virginia 23261-2068

THE ENIGMA OF PERSONALITY

JOURNEY THROUGH THE MIND AND BODY

BY THE EDITORS OF TIME-LIFE BOOKS
ALEXANDRIA, VIRGINIA

CONSULTANTS:

BENNETT G. BRAUN currently directs the section on Psychiatric Trauma at Rush Presbyterian-St. Luke's Medical Center and the Dissociative Disorders Program and Inpatient unit at Rush North Shore Medical Center in Skokie, Illinois.

BARRY M. COHEN, an art therapist, is an expert in psychiatric diagnosis and treatment through art. Much of his work is in the area of multiple personality disorder.

ROBERT A. EMMONS teaches psychology at the University of California, Davis. His major research interest in the area of human motivation focuses on how personal goals relate to emotional, physical, and psychological well-being.

CHARLES F. HALVERSON JR. teaches in the Department of Child and Family Development at the University of Georgia in Athens. A major research interest is relations between parents and children over the life span.

JOHN C. NORCROSS has a clinical practice and is professor of psychology at the University of Scranton. His research examines various theories of psychotherapy and psychotherapy integration.

DON RICHARD RISO, a former Jesuit priest, teaches, writes, and consults on the Enneagram personality type; his works are used as reference texts for Enneagram descriptions and theory.

RICHARD SHWEDER is professor of human development at the University of Chicago. He is a cultural anthropologist and psychologist who studies ethical, emotional, and personality differences among different ethnic groups.

HOWARD TENNEN teaches psychiatry and clinical psychology at the University of Connecticut School of Medicine, Farmington. His research examines how people adapt to threatening events and serious illness. He is editor of the *Journal of Personality*. Tennen was the principal consultant for this volume.

JOURNEY THROUGH THE MIND AND BODY

Time-Life Books is a division of Time Life Inc.

PRESIDENT AND CEO: John M. Fahey Jr.
EDITOR-IN-CHIEF: John L. Papanek

TIME-LIFE BOOKS

MANAGING EDITOR: Roberta Conlan

Executive Art Director: Ellen Robling
Director of Photography and Research: John Conrad Weiser
Senior Editors: Russell B. Adams Jr., Dale M. Brown, Janet Cave, Lee Hassig, Jim Hicks, Robert Somerville, Henry Woodhead
Director of Technology: Eileen Bradley

PRESIDENT: John D. Hall

Vice President, Director of Marketing: Nancy K. Jones
Vice President, New Product Development: Neil Kagan
Director of Production Services: Robert N. Carr
Production Manager: Marlene Zack
Supervisor of Quality Control: James King

Editorial Operations
Production: Celia Beattie
Library: Louise D. Forstall
Computer Composition: Deborah G. Tait (Manager), Monika D. Thayer, Janet Barnes Syring, Lillian Daniels

SERIES EDITOR: Robert Somerville
Administrative Editor: Judith W. Shanks

Editorial Staff for *The Enigma of Personality*
Art Directors: Rebecca Mowrey, Barbara Sheppard, Fatima Taylor
Picture Editor: Tina McDowell
Text Editors: Lee Hassig (principal), Carl Posey, Jim Watson
Associate Editor/Research and Writing: Mark Galan
Associate Editor/Research: Mark Rogers
Assistant Editors/Research: Jennifer Mendelsohn, Narisara Murray
Copyeditor: Donna D. Carey
Editorial Assistants: Kris Dittman, Julia Kendrick
Picture Coordinators: Mark C. Burnett, Paige Henke

Special Contributors:
George Constable, Peter Copeland, Juli Duncan, Laura Foreman, Doug Harbrecht, Gina Maranto, Eliot Marshall, Brian Miller, Peter Pocock, Linda Smith, Mark Washburn (text); Laura Allen, Todd Behrendt, Rebecca Goldsmith, Maureen McHugh, Nathalie op de Beeck, Ann Perry (research); Barbara L. Klein (overread and index); John Drummond (design).

Correspondents:
Elisabeth Kraemer-Singh (Bonn); Otto Gibius, Robert Kroon (Geneva); Christine Hinze (London); Christina Lieberman (New York); Maria Vincenza Aloisi (Paris); Ann Natanson (Rome); Mary Johnson (Stockholm); Dick Berry (Tokyo). Valuable assistance was also provided by Elizabeth Brown, Katheryn White (New York); Dag Christensen (Oslo).

Library of Congress Cataloging-in-Publication Data
The Enigma of Personality/by the editors of Time-Life Books.
p. cm.— (Journey through the mind and body)
Includes bibliographical references and index.
ISBN 0-7835-1008-X (trade)
ISBN 0-7835-1009-8 (library)
1. Personality. I. Time-Life Books. II. Series.
BF698.E665 1994
155.2— dc20 93-44200

© 1994 Time Life Inc. All rights reserved. No part of this book may be reproduced in any form or by any electronic or mechanical means, including information storage and retrieval devices or systems, without prior written permission from the publisher, except that brief passages may be quoted for reviews.
First printing. Printed in U.S.A.
Published simultaneously in Canada.
School and library distribution by Time-Life Education, P.O. Box 85026, Richmond, Virginia 23285-5026.

TIME-LIFE is a trademark of Time Warner Inc. U.S.A.

This volume is one of a series that explores the fascinating inner universe of the human mind and body.

CONTENTS

1

In Pursuit of Psyche

Who has not noticed that some people have sunny dispositions while others always seem gloomy, that some are outgoing and others reserved, that some seem to revel in taking chances while others, inherently more cautious, seek to minimize risk? Such differences between human beings have engrossed psychologists since the earliest days of their science. Some of the giants in the field—men with familiar names such as Sigmund Freud and Carl Jung, as well as others less well known—have devoted much of their lives to penetrating the mystery of human personality: what it is made of; where it comes from; why it can go wrong; and how it can be restored.

The topic of personality attracts attention far beyond the ranks of academic and clinical psychologists. In both the United States and Europe, career changers often use personality tests to guide them in their choice of a new kind of work. Increasingly, employers use such evaluations to help judge whether prospective employees are suited to the work available. Short quizzes dot the pages of certain popular magazines, seeking to shine light into the dim corners of a lover's personality—or a parent's. Individuals often submit to exhaustive assessment in a quest for self-knowledge.

PRECEDING PAGE: A trio of unlike minds, pioneer psychoanalyst Sigmund Freud is flanked by psychologist B. F. Skinner *(right),* who declared that human behavior is shaped by external influences, and humanist Abraham Maslow *(top left),* who believed that all people are governed by a hierarchy of needs.

When personality is not the object of testing, it is often the topic of conversation, as people attempt to describe and understand the behavior of spouses and children, friends and rivals. Along the way, questions arise about which of our predilections we are born with, in what ways we might be shaped by the circumstances of growing up, as well as how different from or similar to each other we really are. Such issues become especially acute with people whose natures, falling outside the broad zone of normality, inflict psychic pain and suffering—not only on themselves but on those around them.

Shelves in bookstores groan under the weight of self-help titles offering all manner of theories about personality, as well as advice for people not overly fond of their own. A recent survey listed more than 400 separate if similar routes to a better self, ranging from the cerebral to the athletic. Ultimately, all such counsel proceeds from either of two much-debated principles. One is that personality, having been well established in most people by their early twenties, is thereafter largely immutable and must somehow be accommodated. The other, conversely, is that personality can always be remade, if not entirely, at least enough that the new self does not continually threaten to resume the ways of the old.

To use a word correctly in a sentence, say semanticists, is to know its meaning. By that measure, most people have a fair idea of what the word *personality* conveys and say it without hesitation to denote a pattern of behavior visible to all. But agreement on the nature of personality tends to evaporate when psychologists of various persuasions attempt to closely examine this everyday definition. Impassioned debate over the precise nature of personality arises, the arguments reflecting differences in philosophy as much as—or more than—they represent differences in science.

Because conclusive evidence to support one view or another is elusive, something of a weed patch of interpretations has grown, some of them complementary and others mutually exclusive. There is one divide, however, that seems historically to force psychologists into one of two groups: those who seek to build a rigorous scientific foundation for understanding personality—and those who tend to see such an approach as wrongheaded and counterproductive.

Modern psychology of personality owes much to Sigmund Freud, despite the controversy that surrounds his work. Born in Austria in 1856 to a middle-class Jewish family, young Sigmund, by his own account, was the "undisputed darling" of his mother, who was 20 years younger than his father. Abandoning dreams of becoming a great general because of anti-Semitism in the military, Freud entered the study of medicine in the 1870s and, upon earning his degree, embarked on a career as a neurophysiologist exploring the anatomy of the brain in a laboratory. Traveling to Paris in 1885, however, Freud spent several months with Jean-Martin Charcot, an early psychiatrist who treated his mentally disturbed patients through hypnosis. Intrigued by the workings of the human mind, Freud soon changed his focus from afflictions of the nervous system to diseases of the psyche.

By the 1890s, Freud's career was shaping up as one of solid achievement but included nothing that would seem to mark him for greatness. Then as he entered middle age, he was pummeled by his own psyche with periodic depressions, apathy, attacks of anxiety, and turbulent mood swings. The death of his father in 1896 only compounded his distress. Not coincidentally, during this period Freud was addicted to cocaine, then valued in some quarters for its supposedly miraculous medicinal qualities. Convinced of its therapeutic value, Freud enthusiastically recommended the drug to friends and patients as a cure for headache.

Today, many of Freud's symptoms are recognized as common effects of cocaine dependence, but Freud believed that the source of his problems lay elsewhere, deep within the recesses of his mind. In 1897, the year after his father's death, Freud began a process of intensive self-analysis, which he continued for the rest of his life. "My recovery," he wrote, "can only come through work in the unconscious; I cannot manage with conscious efforts alone." Thus did Freud begin his celebrated exploration of the inner dynamics of the human personality. He would become perhaps the foremost student of the mind to seek palliatives for others in the exorcism of his own demons.

Freud's view of personality was based on a metaphor that likened the forces of human psychology to water coursing through pipes. If the psychic plumbing was in good working order, a person remained healthy. But if the free flow of "water" was inhibited by, say, the repression of an intense desire in order to avoid adverse consequences of satisfying it, the stream would be blocked. This inhibition or blockage would create the kind of strong feelings of anxiety and other crippling behavior, collectively labeled neuroses, that often spur people into therapy. Freud believed that such blockages resulted from problems in the unconscious mind. They could be removed, he asserted, only by uncovering and understanding the problems through intensive analysis of accidental slips of the tongue, memory lapses, and especially dreams and experiences from early childhood.

Freud interviewed patients using a combination of techniques invented by others, whom he neglected to credit. From a physician friend named Josef Breuer, he borrowed a technique called talking therapy, which Breuer used in treating people for the emotional excitability of hysteria. In this process, Breuer first relaxed such patients through hypnosis, then encouraged them to speak about anything they wished. Looking to Francis Galton, a founder of the London School of Psychology, Freud later added a technique called word association, in which patients were read a list of everyday words—such as head, stalk, ink, paper, nasty, and cow—and were asked to say what first leaped to mind.

Having provided himself with these tools, Freud encouraged his patients to talk about their night dreams and to say anything that came into their minds in response to the dream images. Freud also began to examine his own dreams and his own childhood. Checking his recollections against those of his mother, he came to believe that the roots of his resentment and hostility toward his father and a tendency toward martyrdom, for instance, lay in his repression of affection for his mother.

In 1899 Freud published *The Interpretation of Dreams*, his first book describing his work. Although he later claimed that the psychology establishment ignored the book, it was widely and respectfully reviewed. One reviewer even pronounced it "epoch making." Freud also felt that because his focus on sexuality offended many in his post-Victorian world, adherents of his theory faced persecution and ostracism. In reality, his contemporaries were neither particularly shocked by his probing examination of the human sexual animal, nor notably critical of Freud's followers.

For decades, these and other misrepresentations, picked up and amplified by devotees, helped Freud create and sustain the image of himself as an almost mythical hero battling against the forces of darkness. Indeed, some critics later charged, with ample justification, that the early Freudian circle strongly resembled a

Rorschach's Inkblots: The Beholder's Revealing Eye

It is a common phenomenon to see imaginary figures in the dance of light and shadow or in the mutations of a cloud. To students of the mind, such illusions represent more than mere fancy: What is discerned is, in a sense, a projection of personality, reflecting an individual's experiences and expectations. Recognizing this, Swiss psychiatrist Hermann Rorschach prepared a set of ambiguous images—symmetrical inkblots formed by folding and blotting paper in puddles of ink. He had 300 psychiatric patients and 100 nonpatients interpret the blots, analyzed their responses, and published his results in 1921.

Rorschach's test was little used during his own lifetime, but later it gained wide employment as a diagnostic tool—for example, to evaluate the mental condition of U.S. servicemen returning from World War II. By the 1950s, however, the test had come under fire, with critics charging statistical carelessness in the analysis of patients' interpretations. Nevertheless, the Rorschach test

religious cult, right down to the "excommunication" of followers who dared to disagree with the master's interpretation of the human psyche.

Freud's appreciation of the human condition rested on the idea that society forbids free expression of the two most basic of all human drives: sex and aggression. Thus, from a very early age, he said, people learn to sublimate these energies and to redirect them into channels that are socially acceptable. This inevitably results in a conflict between self and society that threatens to create the kind of psychic blockages that can lead to neurotic behavior.

Human beings normally hold this discord in check through a delicate balancing act among the major components of the psyche, which Freud identified as the id, the ego, and the superego. Primal, instinctive, and unabashedly pleasure seeking, the id is the source of all drive and energy. The judgmental and perfectionist superego resists the id at every turn, punishing its licentious transgressions through guilt and rewarding docility through pride and self-congratulation.

The ego seeks to establish a middle ground between the id's irresponsible hedonist and the superego's strait-laced policeman. Operating through a mechanism that Freud called the reality principle, the ego works to satisfy the wanton demands of the id as far as possible without alerting the superego. More often than not, the ego succeeds by persuading the id to postpone taking its pleasure until a future, more appropriate occasion—that never arrives.

The ebb and flow of this perpetual contest, playing itself out against the backdrop of an individual's childhood experiences, exerts great influence on the personality, according to Freud. In most people, the blockages set up by the delayed gratification of the id merely divert energy into mildly neurotic behavior—the normal complement of anxiety, self-doubt, and occasional benignly compulsive behavior. From time to time, however, the blockages become so great in some people that they cause traumatic distortion of the personality. Freud argued that only by delving into the origins and nature of such blockages—through his combination of talking therapy and free association—could a patient clear the psychic pipes.

In publication after publication, Freud touted psychoanalysis—his term for this technique—as the solution to most of humankind's neuroses. But proof was hard to come by, especially when some of his most celebrated results turned out to be less than he claimed. One famous case involved

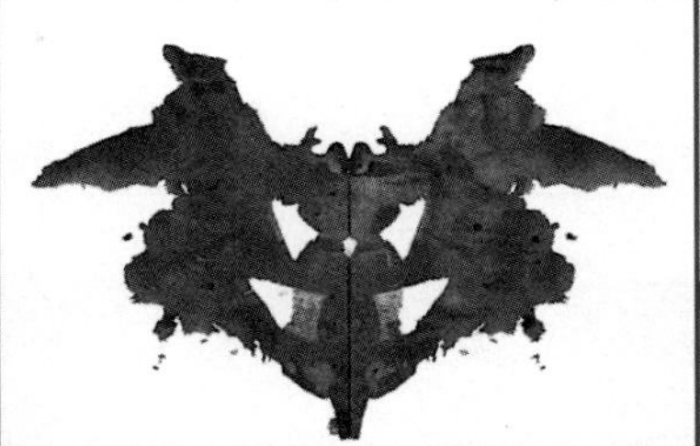

and other variations that have also been developed continue to serve as valuable clinical guides.

What observers see in an inkblot may be less significant than the way they see it. Rorschach established four basic dimensions for interpreting test responses: location, organization, determinants, and content. Location refers to how much of a blot and which parts of blots the subject uses to make interpretations. In a series of blots, for example, consistently looking at one area rarely selected by other subjects may suggest a tendency to focus on the unusual—a sign of either creative individuality or perhaps an inability to follow conventional thought processes. Rorschach's organization dimension assesses how well the subject sees the world in complex terms. Determinants indicate whether the subject sees only shape, or color, texture, and movement as well. And content is a measure of the subject's tendency to interpret the blots as recognizable objects.

a young man who suffered from depression and other psychological difficulties. Interviewing the patient, Freud learned that, as a child, he had witnessed intercourse between his parents and subsequently dreamed a terrifying nightmare involving several white wolves lurking outside his window. In a thoroughgoing analysis, Freud linked the two experiences with the young man's neuroses, explaining among other things that the color of the wolves' fur mimicked the white of the parents' undergarments.

Freud treated the Wolf Man, as he called him, through psychoanalysis and, after four years, pronounced him cured. The case was hailed as a triumph of psychoanalytic theory and practice. But in an extensive interview conducted 60 years later, the Wolf Man reported that he had continued to suffer from the same symptoms throughout his life. "You know I feel so bad, I have been having such terrible depressions lately," the Wolf Man told the interviewer. "You probably think that psychoanalysis didn't do me any good," giving words to a thought held by many of Freud's critics.

Contrary to his own advice, Freud even reached a diagnosis without extensive or thorough psychoanalysis. Such was the 1908 case of a five-year-old Viennese boy—Little Hans, as he came to be known—who one day suddenly developed an aversion to going outdoors for fear that he would be bitten by a horse. Relying mostly upon the testimony from the little boy's father, who enthusiastically agreed with Freud's theories, Freud saw the child just once before arriving at an explanation for the problem: The horse, with its big penis, represented the father, and Hans's fear of being bitten related to castration anxiety.

Freud saw the boy's fear as an expression of something that the psychiatrist called the Oedipus complex, named for Oedipus, the tragic hero of Greek legend who unwittingly slept with his mother and killed his father. "Hans," wrote Freud, "was really a little Oedipus who wanted his father 'out of the way', so that he might be alone with his handsome mother and sleep with her." This unresolved oedipal conflict was the source of Hans's sudden phobia about horses.

After these complicated insights were explained to Little Hans, the phobia disappeared—seemingly a ringing confirmation of Freudian theory and the efficacy of psychoanalysis. But there was more to the story. Later it came to light that shortly before

the onset of his apprehension, Hans had witnessed a traffic accident involving a horse and a tram. "When the horse and the bus fell down," Hans recounted some months later, "it gave me such a fright, really! That was when I got the nonsense," which gradually went away.

Perhaps most surprising, given Freud's endorsement of talking therapy and free association, is his invention of psychohistory, a concept by which he sought to analyze historical figures by examining artifacts they had left behind. In 1910 he wrote a book that attempted a psychohistorical analysis of Leonardo da Vinci.

Although virtually nothing was known about Leonardo da Vinci's upbringing, Freud managed to extract great meaning from a short note the artist and inventor had scribbled on the back of some of his sketches of birds. In the note, Leonardo mentioned that one of his earliest memories involved a vulture coming to land on his cradle and brushing its wings against his mouth.

From this tiny nugget—and citing the fact that the Egyptian hieroglyphs for "mother" and "vulture" were identical—Freud professed to reconstruct Leonardo da Vinci's entire childhood. Interpreting the vulture story as fantasy rather than fact, he asserted that the young genius had been forsaken by his father and raised by his mother—the vulture in his fantasy—all of which, asserted Freud, led to homosexual tendencies.

It is true that at age 24 Leonardo was accused anonymously of homosexuality and acquitted. However, even a guilty verdict would not patch the many flaws in Freud's analysis. They begin with the questionable connection between Egyptian hieroglyphs—which had not yet been deciphered—and what Freud presented as the Florentine artist's unconscious association of his mother with a vulture. Furthermore, the psychiatrist was victimized by a mistranslation as "vulture" of the Italian word for a kite, a small hawk with no particular significance in mythologies of the Nile. For all that, however, the overriding objection of many, not only to psychohistory but to psychoanalysis in general, was a simple one: The results were either unverifiable, for Leonardo da Vinci, or specious, as in the cases of the Wolf Man and Little Hans.

Such a poor harvest raised questions about the theoretical underpinnings of psychoanalysis, about the blockages and energy diversion, and about the weight given by Freud to dreams and childhood experiences as keys to personality. However grand, universal, and satisfying Freud's psychoanalytic theory may have been to many, it had a chameleon-like quality of transforming itself to accommodate any result or of selectively ignoring the facts. For example, when confronted with the vulture-kite error in the Leonardo analysis, Freud's followers dismissed the confusion as merely an awkward detail. Equally inadequate excuses were made in the cases of Little Hans, the Wolf Man, and others.

The impossibility of testing Freud's ideas rankled many of his critics, who held that a scientific theory must be able to be proved false by future observations. The longer such data do not turn up, the more standing the theory gains as a plausible description of reality. The hypothesis that all crows are black, for example, is easily refuted by anyone showing up with an albino crow. But Freud's constructs—the id, ego, and superego—allowed no possibility of proof or disproof. Whenever critics thought they noticed a psychoanalytic white crow among the black, Freudians simply redefined their concepts. Mindful of this, the great German philosopher of science Karl Popper lumped psychoanalysis together with astrology and other unprovable concepts, considering it nothing more than pseudoscience.

Yet all the criticism, however justified, cannot erase Freud's considerable accomplishment in establishing a language that allowed for meaningful discussion of human personality. Many of Freud's concepts—repression and sublimation, for example—have become useful parts of everyday vocabulary. And his concepts of the id, ego, and superego have found widespread acceptance as a metaphor of the internal conflicts that beset most of the human race from time to time.

Freud's place in history is secure, but by 1970 his theory had fallen into disfavor among many former enthusiasts. Much of his work was relegated to the realm of philosophy and speculation rather than science. One who was squarely in the scientific camp, by contrast, was American psychologist John B. Watson. Born in 1878, two decades after Freud, Watson preferred to use animals rather than human subjects in his experiments. "With animals," he wrote, "I was at home. I was keeping close to biology with my feet on the ground."

Watson coined the term *behaviorism* to describe what was to become a major new school of psychology. In a 1914 article, Watson wrote: "Psychology as the behaviorist views it is a purely objective experimental branch of natural science." Rather than relying on untestable theoretical constructs and introspective analysis by probing a human subject's dreams

and childhood anxieties, behaviorists believed that they could learn more about psychology by directly observing and measuring the responses of laboratory animals. From there, the behaviorists maintained, it would be easy to extrapolate the results to human beings. "The behaviorist," wrote Watson, "recognizes no dividing line between man and brute."

Watson was teaching at Johns Hopkins University in Baltimore during the second decade of the 20th century when he learned of some intriguing experiments conducted by Ivan Petrovich Pavlov. The Russian physiologist had discovered that he could condition dogs—train them—to salivate in response to the sound of a bell or some other stimulus in anticipation of food, even when none was present or forthcoming. Of particular interest to Watson, however, were Pavlov's later experiments. In them, the Russian learned that he could elicit odd behavior in a dog trained, say, to salivate when presented with a drawing of a circle but not to salivate when shown an ellipse. If then shown an almost circular ellipse, the dog would begin to squeal and bark and bite at the experimental apparatus, canine equivalents of a neurotic level of frustration in human beings.

Pavlov's work dovetailed perfectly with Watson's equation between "man and brute." If neurotic behavior could arise in animals, not as a result of long-repressed instincts but in the controlled environment of a laboratory, then why not in humans, too?

Returning from service in World War I, Watson abandoned his rule against using human subjects and began a series of experiments with infants. He and his graduate assistant, Rosalie Rayner, conducted a behaviorist experiment expressly designed to tweak the Freudians and that today would not pass ethical muster. Working with 11-month-old Little Albert, whose mother granted permission for the venture, Watson and Rayner presented the baby with a white rat and then struck a hammer against a metal bar, producing a loud, jarring clang. Very soon, Little Albert began to cry at the very appearance of the rat, even without the unpleasant noise. In a short time, Watson and Rayner had generalized Albert's "conditioned emotional reaction" to include all small, furry animals.

One of several Skinner box designs, this particular apparatus includes a mechanism that delivers food to a hungry laboratory rat when it presses a bar in its compartment. Skinner's devices were intended to demonstrate that behavior does not spring from any kind of subjective or emotional state, but merely represents a learned response to a stimulus that is either reinforced by a reward or inhibited by a punishment.

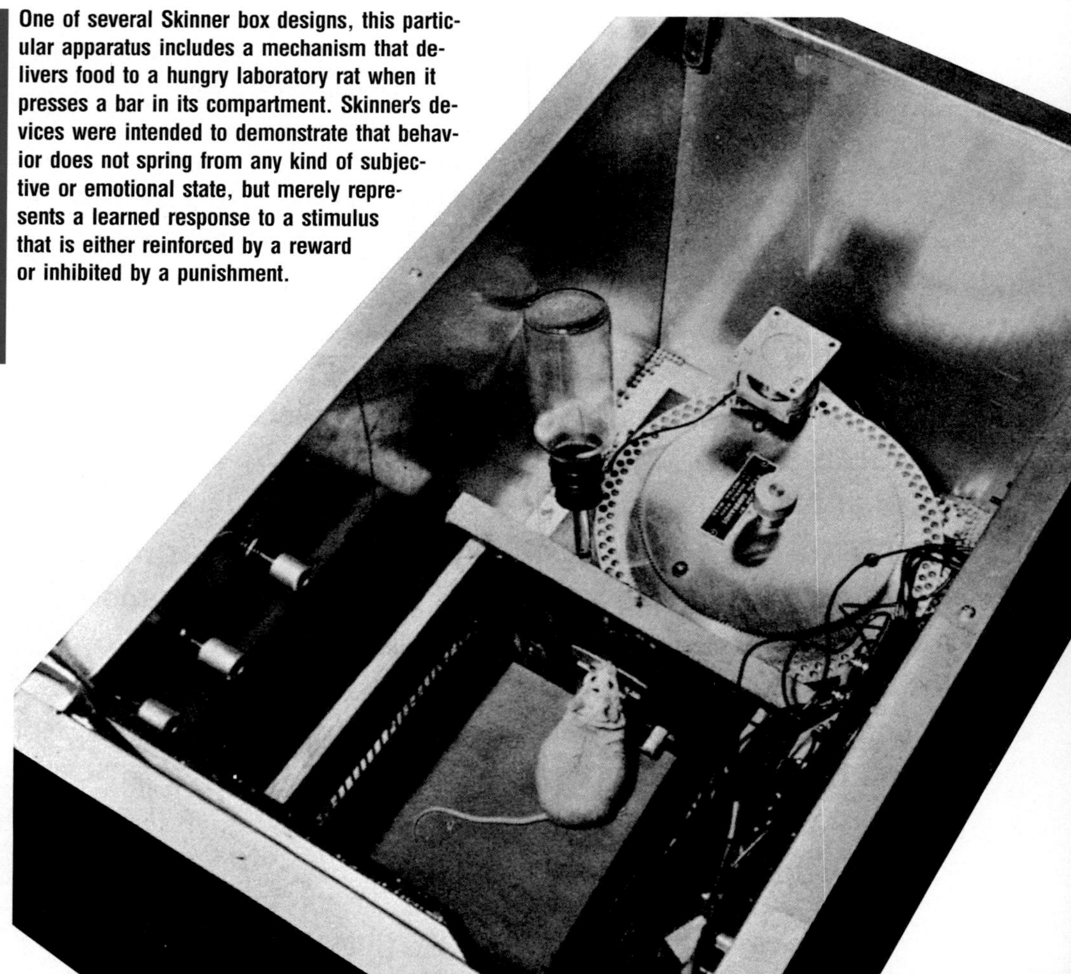

Any contest between Little Albert's nascent id and superego, it seemed, was irrelevant. His neurotic fear of small animals—essentially indistinguishable from Little Hans's fear of horses—was purely a learned response to an external stimulus. Watson taunted the Freudians by suggesting that if Albert were to undergo psychoanalysis 20 years later, the analyst would probably conclude that Albert's deep-seated fear had been brought on by sexually oriented childhood experiences, revealed through the interpretation of dreams.

Watson's research with infants came to a halt when his behavior outside the lab brought a premature end to his career as a research psychologist. In 1920 he divorced his wife and married Rayner, his graduate-student assistant. The ensuing scandal forced him to resign his post at Johns Hopkins, and he spent the rest of his working life in the advertising business where, he later wrote, "I began to learn that it can be just as thrilling to watch the growth of a sales curve of a new product as to watch the learning curve of animals or men." And there is this footnote tinged with both tragedy and irony: Watson raised his two sons in accordance with his behaviorist theories of stimulus and response. One son committed suicide; the other became a psychoanalyst.

Some 15 years after Watson left Johns Hopkins, the behaviorist banner was picked up and carried to new heights by Burrhus Frederic (B. F.) Skinner. Born in 1904 to a strait-laced attorney and his domineering wife, young Skinner was, in his words, "taught to fear God, the police, and what people will think." As a youth, he developed an inventor's interest in things mechanical. He once made a sign, for example, that reminded him to hang up his bathrobe—and rigged the notice to disappear when he did so. After a failed attempt to become a novelist, Skinner went through a period of depression, in the midst of which he read *Behaviorism*, a book about Watson's work written by the defrocked scientist himself and published in 1930. Inspired, Skinner went on to study psychology and soon thereafter became behaviorism's most outspoken and prominent champion.

Skinner found the very concept of "personality" to be irrelevant and misleading. As far as he was concerned, animal behavior—whether the animal was a rat, a pigeon, or a human—was no more than the accumulation of learned responses to external stimuli. Eschewing subjective concepts such as wishes and emotions, Skinner spoke of stimuli as reward or punishment. A reward tends to encourage a response; punishment inhibits. In the right combinations, reinforcement could spark or quench any behavior imaginable.

To Pavlov's basic concept of stimulus and response, Skinner added the idea of initiative. That is, an animal need not depend on stimulus and reinforcement supplied by the experimenter; it could learn to provide its own, as when a laboratory rat figures out how to push a button in order to receive a food pellet. Operant conditioning was the name that Skinner gave this voluntary behavior, in which a subject could "operate" on the environment to produce a result.

In contrast to Freud's cerebral theorizing, Skinner's animal experiments seemed to offer a scientific method for exploring virtually any sort of behavior, including those generally considered to constitute personality. Not only could behavior be observed and measured, but the experiments in one lab could be duplicated in others and the results compared. In other words, Skinner's methods contained the means of proving or refuting any psychological hypothesis. These pluses won Skinner a wide following as other psychologists devised their own behaviorist experiments. Soon, in laboratories throughout the world, legions of rats were diligently pressing levers and buttons in "Skinner boxes" (*page* 16) in order to get food pellets or to avoid shocks.

To many people, however, the idea of behaviorism was profoundly disturbing. By denying any difference between animals and human beings, the theory seemed to open the door to the frightening possibility that men, women, and children were little more than living clay, ready for molding by any evil genius. The specter was seized on by more than one novelist. In George Orwell's 1984, for example, everyman Winston Smith's rebellion against the oppressive Big Brother is ruthlessly conditioned into extinction, and in the chilling conclusion, Smith learns to love the totalitarian system that he had tried to bring down. In Anthony Burgess's novel *A Clockwork Orange*, the hapless, if vicious, protagonist falls into the clutches of a behaviorist who, through Pavlovian conditioning, deliberately turns the young rebel's greatest source of pleasure—the music of Beethoven—into a source of pain.

As it happened, by the 1960s behaviorism had become somewhat tempered. Further research had revealed that the lab animals varied in their responses to test stimuli. In one conditioning experiment, for instance, rats were irradiated with x-rays to make them nauseated after drinking water that was either sugared or accompanied by a loud noise or bright light. The animals soon learned to avoid illness by refusing the sweetened water, but they persisted in drinking the "loud" and "bright" water even though they got sick afterward.

This and other examples stood as evidence that each species is more responsive to some stimuli than to others. As two researchers expressed it in the 1960s, "Learned behavior drifts toward instinctive behavior." Thus, the reactions of rats and monkeys could not be reliably extrapolated to human beings. Skinner and his predecessor John Watson may have drawn no distinction between man and brute, but nature apparently does.

At about the time that John Watson was teaching Little Albert to fear small animals, a fresh idea about personality was taking shape in the thinking of Swiss psychiatrist Carl Jung, the most prominent of the early Freudian circle. Born in 1875, Jung had flirted with philosophy and archaeology before turning to the study of medicine and then falling under Freud's influence. Although he was anointed by the master as his successor, Jung broke with his mentor in 1912, citing Freud's overemphasis on sex.

Between 1914 and 1917, Jung—like many other great physicians of the mind—underwent a period of crisis, sinking into depression and near-madness. He emerged from his trials with new insights on the nature of human beings. Soon his writings won him a large and devoted following.

Taking an important first step toward a strict scientific theory of personality, Jung proposed that there might be just a few basic kinds of people. In *Psychological Types*, published in 1921, the psychiatrist identified two fundamentally different psychological styles, which he labeled extraversion and introversion. Extraversion, he wrote, "is characterized by interest in the external object, responsiveness, and a ready acceptance of external happenings, a desire to influence and be influenced by events, a need to join in and get 'with it.' " The introverted personality, on the other hand, "holds aloof from external happenings, does not join in, has a distinct dislike of society and is not in the least 'with it.' " Jung further predicted that introverts who happened to become neurotic would tend to suffer from anxiety and related problems, whereas extraverts would develop so-called hysterical neuroses often characterized by psychosomatic pains and illnesses.

Jung took care to point out that he was not engaged in idle list making. Although not a behaviorist, he was troubled by the imprecision of hypotheses offered by the young science of psychology and their inability to be tested. "Someday," Jung wrote, "psychologists will have to agree upon certain basic principles if psychology is not to remain an unscientific conglomeration of individual opinions." Jung intended his ideas of extraversion and introversion to be his contribution to a testable theory of human personality. No experimenter himself, Jung challenged others to confirm his typology in the lab, then turned to other topics. Much of his writing after *Psychological Types* dealt with notions on such philosophical concepts as the collective unconscious, by which he meant the part of the subconscious that all humans share. Before he died in 1961, he wrote about subjects as arcane as astrology, alchemy, telepathy, and flying saucers.

The way to test Jung's theory was to convert his descriptions of introverts and extraverts into objective criteria and apply them to many individuals. If any of the subjects did not conform to either type, Jung's theory could be shown false and modified accordingly. Like Freud, Jung had many followers and advocates in the world of psychology, but they were, for the most part, no more experimenters than he.

So the initial exploration of introversion and its opposite fell to a self-described behaviorist and committed anti-Freudian by the name of Hans J. Eysenck. A young British psychologist working at a military mental institution in the mid-1940s, Eysenck performed a complex statistical analysis of the case histories of some 700 disturbed patients. He found that the more neurotic among his subjects largely fell into the anxious and hysterical groups forecast by Jung for his two types of personality.

So far, Eysenck had found evidence for only half of Jung's theory. Next, he scoured psychological literature for some evidence to support Jung's hypothesis that introversion would be linked to anxiety and extraversion to hysteria. He came upon it in the work of psychologists who had evaluated scores of neurotic individuals. Analysis of the results amply demonstrated the strong connection that Eysenck was looking for.

Eysenck not only confirmed the fundamentals of Jung's typology but expanded upon and made refinements to it as well. Introversion and extraversion, he realized, could be seen as opposite ends of a single line, or dimension. A personality could fall anywhere along the line and be typed accordingly. But Eysenck's studies suggested to him that two additional dimensions were necessary to explain his observations. He gathered evidence to show that, regardless of their placement on the introvert-extravert scale, people could also be more neurotic or less so—as well as solidly connected to reality or not, a dimension that he called psychoticism.

Although originally a behaviorist, Eysenck theorized that introversion and extraversion were not conditioned responses at all, but inborn temperaments; the absence in his research of a correlation between an individual's life experience and his or her position on this dimension suggested as much. Instead, Eysenck speculated that extraversion and introversion somehow were influenced by differences in the workings of the brain. Introverts, he proposed, might have high levels of internal mental arousal; consequently, they would tend through reticence to minimize additional arousal. Extraverts would be just the opposite—seeking external stimulation to balance low levels of the internal variety.

Once again, dogs had shown the way. Pavlov found that he could place his test animals on an extraversion scale virtually identical to the one for humans proposed independently by

Carl Jung. The affable, happy-go-lucky canines were the extraverts; quiet, reserved animals were the introverts. Beyond that, the Russian physiologist discovered that introverted dogs remained alert throughout the experiment and were therefore more easily conditioned than their extraverted brethren, who often became bored with the proceedings and fell asleep. Furthermore, suggested Pavlov, the introverted animals remained attentive because for them the experiment represented enough external stimulation added to their natural state of arousal to keep them alert. In extraverted animals, however, the conditioning process provided too little stimulus to jolt them out of their naturally lower state of arousal. Learning of Pavlov's findings, Eysenck extrapolated them from dogs to humans.

In the early 1950s, Cyril Franks, a psychologist at Princeton University in New Jersey, conducted a number of experiments that would help to substantiate Eysenck's theory. Human research subjects received Pavlovian conditioning to a tone followed by a puff of air aimed at the eye; subsequently, occurrences of eye blinks produced by the tone when unaccompanied by an air puff were counted as a measure of the degree of conditioning. Just like the dogs, subjects who had been typed as introverts were indeed found to be more easily and successfully conditioned than those typed as extraverts.

These results were bolstered by studies of the brain itself. Electroencephalographs measuring electrical activity in the brain showed that different individuals have different levels of internal mental arousal, which accounts in part for their positions along the introversion-extraversion dimension. Franks's and other experiments supported Eysenck's hypothesis that behavior and personality are produced by an interaction between social forces and inherited genetic predispositions.

The full complexity of Eysenck's theories is difficult for all but the most studious to penetrate. Yet in every detail, he specifically designed his model of personality dimensions to pass the refutability test of good science. Indeed, when Franks's experiments turned up some flaws in his reasoning, Eysenck willingly made revisions in his theory to acknowledge the unexpected findings. Wrote Eysenck: "I have sometimes said, only half in jest, that my model of personality is the only one on the market that can claim to have been experimentally disconfirmed; this is a source of pride, not of regret."

Perhaps so, but Eysenck's typology did not turn out to be the unifying concept of personality that he might reasonably have expected it to become. Freudians, persevering in the language of id, ego, and superego, could see little point in applying the scientific method to the psyche. Behaviorists, who continued to think of the environment as the primary influence on individuality, viewed Eysenck's personality types as frills at best, insisting that animals remain the sum of their responses to external stimuli, whatever names might be proposed for the phenomenon.

Eysenck, however, seemed something of a kindred spirit to the adherents of yet another school of thought on the subject of personality: trait psychology. The originator of trait psychology in the mid-1930s was Harvard-educated psychologist Gordon Allport, who looked to language more than to behavior as a source of enlightenment about personality. Allport believed that ordinary human beings were skilled observers of personality and that the words in their languages that described people's traits provided the best clues to their nature and variety. Intent on assembling a complete list of such characteristics, he and colleague Henry Odbert pored through an English-language dictionary and extracted a catalog of every word related to personality, some

Helping the Mind Tell Stories on Itself

The two women in the enigmatic image above are intended to evoke feelings about mother figures. They are part of a larger cast of probing characters designed to uncover human drives, anxieties, wishes, and conflicts through the Thematic Apperception Test, or TAT, a method of evaluating patients' psyches first introduced by psychologist Henry A. Murray in 1943. Like the Rorschach, Murray's TAT relies on deliberately ambiguous images—in this case, a series of 20 picture cards showing human figures—to elicit personality-exposing responses. But the TAT asks for more than a quick reaction to what the eye sees: Subjects must make up detailed stories to explain the scene. In the course of creating characters and situations, they often reveal themselves as they could not, or would not, under direct questioning.

Several studies have confirmed that the cards help show how much of an effect real-life experiences and different cultural settings can have on a person's outlook. In the 1980s, for example, when a group of immigrants from war-torn Central America were given the test, they told stories of torture and death to go with pictures that had been given innocuous interpretations by North Americans. The test also revealed subtle cultural differences in adult-child relationships and attitudes toward achievement. Card 1, a picture of a boy contemplating a violin, reminded North Americans of being prodded by parents to practice; the Central Americans created scenarios of a child eager to seek help in learning how to play.

Mindfarers: Exploring the Terra Incognita of the Self

18,000 in all. By weeding out synonyms and words that, upon further consideration, had little to say about personality, he later condensed the list to fewer than 5,000 entries.

In perusing the list, Allport noted that many of the personality traits could be paired as opposites—aggressive with submissive, for example—known as complements. Although most people fell in the middle of such a scale, a person might tend toward one end or the other depending on the circumstances. Almost anyone, he argued, would find occasions in life that called for a higher-than-usual degree of assertiveness and others that demanded a greater measure of acquiescence.

For Allport, individual personalities could comprise a large number of traits. In relatively uncommon individuals, something that he called a cardinal trait would appear, a characteristic that is so strong and consistent that it eclipses the others. Most people, however, possess a few prominent but not overpowering characteristics—central traits, Allport called them—by which they are known. Additionally, there were a number of secondary traits that surface rarely and often pass unnoticed except by the person's closest acquaintances.

As appealing and sensible as Allport's description of personality may sound, in the eyes of some critics trait psychology embodies a fault of logic known as circular reasoning, in which one statement leads to another that is used as proof for the first. For example, sentimental behavior observed in a person is assumed to be one of the individual's personality traits, which is then cited as the source or cause of the sentimentality—that is, someone is emotional because he or she is, well, emotional.

Undaunted by such objections, however, an army of psychologists buckled down to the task of turning Allport's pile of carefully selected straws into the gold of real science. In the decades following World War II, proponents of the trait theory devised thousands of personality tests that tried to categorize the traits of individuals. The results of these tests yielded to the same kind of statistical analysis that Eysenck used. As they continued their study, the list of traits shrank, first in a big jump from 4,580 entries to 171 and then to 35 during the mid-1940s. Next it went to 12 and finally, in 1963, to only five.

Exhaustive testing and analysis reduced the number no further, and by the 1980s, trait psychologists had settled on something they called the Five Factor Model of personality.

Thinned from so many to so few, Allport's traits seem not all that different in principle from Eysenck's dimensions, the more so because the Five Factor Model includes two of them: neuroticism and introversion-extraversion. The other three factors are commonly labeled openness to experience, agreeableness, and conscientiousness (*pages* 32-33). Within each of these factors fall a handful of subordinate traits that represent consistent patterns of thoughts, feelings, and actions. Three of the seven complementary pairs of traits under agreeableness, for example, are: suspicious and trusting; stingy and generous; and irritable and good-natured.

The Five Factor Model appeals to a great many personality psychologists. With only a limited number of dimensions, it possesses a refreshing economy of means compared with the nearly 5,000 traits enumerated by Allport. Furthermore, the Five Factor Model seems more complete than Eysenck's and other measures of personality in wide use, better able to encompass the entire range of nuance found in human personality. Although these findings do not constitute incontrovertible evidence for the Five Factor Model of personality, they have persuaded many psychologists that it is probably a useful theory.

Of course, not everyone agrees. Some see the Five Factor Model, as

SIGMUND FREUD probed his own unconscious to reveal the sexually preoccupied mind described in such works as the groundbreaking *Interpretation of Dreams,* published in 1899.

IVAN PAVLOV set the stage for the behaviorist school with his experiments on dogs in the early 1900s, which showed that behavior could be shaped through so-called conditioning.

well as the underlying linguistic approach that Allport and Odbert pioneered with their journey through the dictionary, as not in the least revealing of personality. First, single words and even complementary pairs fall short of describing some aspects of personality, say these critics. Beyond that, the critics say, Allport's central assumption—that everything about personality can be dug out of language as it has evolved—necessarily leads to circular reasoning that no amount of statistical analysis of traits can straighten out. To borrow from the field of computer science: Garbage in, garbage out. Skeptics go on to point out that the Five Factor Model's exhaustive classification of personality ignores what goes on inside each individual that gives rise to the very thing it professes to catalog.

Whatever the outcome of the debate, it will entirely miss the point, according to another group of psychologists. Known as humanists, they frown upon not only the Five Factor Model, Hans Eysenck, and the behaviorists, but the Freudian school as well. To humanists, all these groups have a common flaw: They see people as prisoners of their past, whether that implies genetic inheritances, conditioned responses, childhood traumas, or other forces.

Gordon Allport, the pioneer of trait psychology, was also one of the first in his field to assert that people can transcend such formidable influences. "Personality," he wrote, "is becoming, not merely being." Allport contended that people never stop striving to become the person they want to be, to fulfill their sense of self.

Allport was not alone in this opinion. One of his contemporaries in the late 1930s, a young student of psychology named Abraham Maslow, thought that psychologists spent too much energy studying damaged psyches. It made much more sense, thought Maslow, to study healthy personalities, especially those of people—self-actualized, he called them—who had freed themselves from the

CARL JUNG, once a Freud devotee, proposed his own theory of personality in 1921, categorizing people according to a few distinct types —among them extraverts and introverts.

B. F. SKINNER asserted in the 1930s that human behavior consists merely of responses to external stimuli; he devised an assortment of experimental equipment to test his ideas.

psychological bonds implied by all the theories of personality then brewing. Rather than studying the worst that humanity had to offer, Maslow was determined to investigate the best of the breed, and by 1954, he had collected his thoughts about personality into a book titled *Motivation and Personality*.

To Maslow, a self-actualized person was one who has followed the philosopher Nietzsche's exhortation to "Become what thou art!" The concept of self-actualization, according to Maslow, "may be loosely described as the full use and exploitation of talents, capacities, potentialities, etc. Such people seem to be fulfilling themselves and to be doing the best that they are capable of doing."

The key to personality, Maslow believed, lay in motivations, or needs—and how a person went about satisfying them—rather than in the genes or in childhood experiences. To flesh out the idea, Maslow identified a hierarchy of necessities, which served the function of organizing and integrating life experiences. At the most basic level, human beings must satisfy physiological needs, such as food, water, sleep, and sex. At the second level, there is the pursuit of safety. The third level centers on the quest for love; the fourth on the need for self-respect and the esteem of others. Beyond these basic motivations, there are higher levels that only self-actualized persons seem able to fulfill—the thirst for truth, beauty, and justice.

For most individuals, progress toward self-actualization requires the satisfaction of the needs at each successive level. If a person is hungry, self-esteem is irrelevant. If someone feels unloved, the quest for justice will have to wait. Most people never advance to the upper levels of the hierarchy but spend their lives trying to cope with basic needs. However, a few exceptional people, Maslow noted, seem to leap directly to the high plateau; great artists and musicians, for example, may not object much to living in poverty or may place little value on the esteem of others. In skipping the early steps toward self-actualization, such individuals usually have semimystical

GORDON ALLPORT rejected Freud's premise that adults are prisoners of infantile drives; his 1930s trait theory focused instead on how a combination of attributes form personality.

HANS EYSENCK, based on his analysis of soldiers in World War II, enlarged on Jung's extravert and introvert types to include the concepts of neuroticism and psychoticism.

ABRAHAM MASLOW wrote in the 1950s that an individual's personality reflects a continual effort to satisfy a hierarchy of needs—a process he called self-actualization.

peak experiences in which they obtain a glimpse of some transcendent truth. Among those whom Maslow considered likely self-actualizers were prominent individuals such as Abraham Lincoln, Eleanor Roosevelt, and Adlai Stevenson.

Anyone, thought Maslow, may have a peak experience. More often than not, however, it does not lead to a state of self-actualization, because most people tend to deny the significance of those valuable moments. They "desacralize" them, he said, thereby denying the awesome and sublime aspects of the universe to focus instead on fulfilling lower-order needs. Maslow considered much of scientific psychology to be an attempt to desacralize humanity itself.

In contrast to the categorizers, the typologists, and the experimenters, Maslow's views were deliberately vague: "If humanistic science may be said to have any goals beyond sheer fascination with the human mystery and enjoyment of it, these would be to release the person from external controls and make him less predictable to the observer (to make him freer, more creative, more inner-determined) even though perhaps more predictable to himself."

Maslow has been joined in this humanist approach by a substantial cadre of psychologists who also wish to affirm the human potential for change. In doing so, however, they take a step away from science founded upon theories that can be tested. Humanist predictions about personality are generally so ambiguous that they could accommodate any outcome of any experiment intended to verify them. "Maslow's study of self-actualizing individuals," wrote psychologist Robert Ewen, "defines such people subjectively, using his own personal criteria. It has been suggested that the behaviors he characterizes as ideal (and even the hierarchy of needs itself) represent not some fundamental truth, but his own idiosyncratic conception of what human values should be like." The same could be said of many philosophers.

In rebuttal, humanists tend to argue that a purely scientific approach to understanding personality has serious flaws of its own. As Gordon Allport once objected, it breaks the concept into components but never reintegrates it. So personality is never seen as it appears in real people. Arguing in effect that the whole is greater than the sum of its parts, humanists contend that a somewhat fuzzy appreciation of the entire personality is superior to more precise knowledge of isolated elements.

Clearly, there is much honest disagreement about the nature of personality. Furthermore, the various perspectives evolve constantly. Freudians, although they continue to delve into a person's past for insights, no longer speak so exclusively of the id, the ego, and the superego. Proponents of the more rigorously scientific views of personality, with roots in Carl Jung and extending to the Five Factor Model, continue to refine their analyses. Behaviorists have retreated somewhat from their hard-line, pure stimulus-response stance. They now concede that human beings are far more than mere leaves swirling helplessly in the winds of stimuli; in fact, people actually think about their circumstances—and in doing so they affect their own behavior.

Some observers suspect that the quest to achieve a complete understanding of personality may be doomed to eternal frustration. It is almost as if personality were a fantastic sculpture, ornate with apertures and appendages. Psychologists trying to describe it in the light of different theories see only the shadows it casts. While each shadow may embody a particle of truth, all of them together may never reveal all there is to know about human personality. Yet psychologists press ever forward in their engrossing quest to understand not only what constitutes personality, but where it comes from, in what ways it goes awry, and whether, once established, it can be altered a little, a lot, or not at all.

CATEGORIZING CHARACTER

The human urge to measure and define everything from the atom to the cosmos itself applies with no less vigor in the realms of personality. Beginning in ancient times and continuing to the present day, observers have attempted to identify the components of character and then use that knowledge to classify individuals into a variety of distinct types. Indeed, most of us can recognize in ourselves a tendency to label the people we know.

The following pages describe three established methods for typing personality, each relying on different strategies for defining traits and, in the end, arriving at different classification schemes. To some extent, each differs in its purpose as well, emphasizing similarities between types, or differences, or focusing more on the role of specific traits. But they all share the goal of enabling individuals to see themselves—their strengths and their weaknesses—more clearly.

Enlightened practitioners of such techniques, though still espousing the value of typecasting individuals, as it were, recognize that no such approach can reach into all the intimate spaces of a human life. Ultimately, they agree, each one of us is unique.

The Enneagram's nine personality types fall into three groups *(colored segments at right)*, known as the Feeling *(blue)*, Doing *(black)*, and Relating *(purple)* Triads. Each type in a group exhibits either strength or weakness in the group's fundamental attribute. Lines connecting the types reveal additional relationships, indicating the other kinds of person an individual may become through psychological growth or deterioration. The unhealthy traits of a Peacemaker, for example, might lead a person to become a Loyalist, while the healthy traits could turn someone into a Motivator.

NEW LIFE FOR AN AGE-OLD SYMBOL

The Enneagram—a nine-pointed figure (from the Greek word *ennea*, or "nine") that serves to represent personality types and the relationships between them—probably originated in Babylon or elsewhere in the Middle East as long ago as 2500 BC, although its precise origins are unknown. Some scholars trace the enneagram to the numerological discoveries of ancient mathematicians that were later adopted and applied to studies of the self by secret orders of the Islamic mystics known as Sufis, perhaps around the 14th or 15th century AD.

Unheard of in the West before the 20th century, the Enneagram began to reach a wider audience in the United States in the 1970s. The chart is now often taught in seminars and used as a tool for psychological evaluations.

The theory on which the Enneagram is based posits nine basic personality types, each encompassing traits that are characterized as healthy, average, or unhealthy for that type. For instance, in type 8, or the Leader, self-confidence is a healthy trait and a tendency to be domineering an unhealthy one. Individuals differ in the mix of these traits and the degree to which they are expressed.

The Enneagram itself shows how the various types are related and the ways in which, according to the theory, personality can change. The lines on the diagram connect each type with two others, one of which represents a positive change from the original type, the other a negative.

9

THE PEACEMAKER
The easygoing, accommodating type. Accepting, good-natured, and trusting, peacemakers can also be too willing to go along with others. Creatures of habit, they can be passive and stubborn. At their best, peacemakers are able to bring people together and resolve conflicts.

1

THE REFORMER
The rational, idealistic type. Reformers are conscientious, with a strong sense of ethics. Always trying to improve things, they are also afraid of making mistakes. Well organized and neat, they can be impersonal and rigid. At their best, reformers are noble and morally heroic.

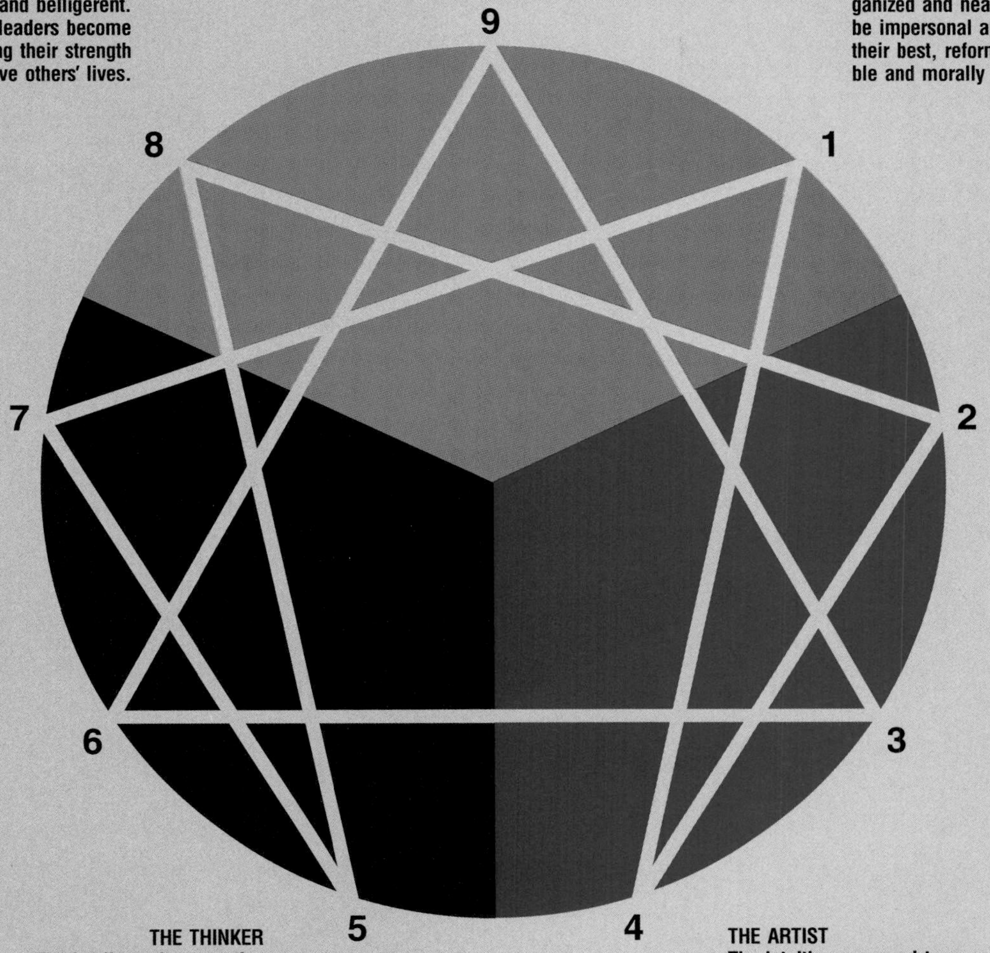

2

THE HELPER
The caring, nurturing type. Helpers are people oriented and self-sacrificing. Generous and warm, they can also be intrusive and overly sentimental. Possessive of others, they may have hidden agendas. At their best, helpers are altruistic and capable of unconditional love.

3

THE MOTIVATOR
The adaptable, success-oriented type. Motivators are self-assured and charming. Energetic and ambitious, they can become too driven and competitive. At their worst, they can be opportunistic and slick. At their best, motivators are true role models who inspire others.

4

THE ARTIST
The intuitive, reserved type. Artists are introspective, sensitive, and gentle. Emotionally honest and personal, artists can also be moody and self-conscious. At times, they may become melancholy and consumed by fantasy. At their best, artists are highly creative people.

5

THE THINKER
The intellectual, perceptive type. Thinkers concentrate well and understand complex ideas. Curious and inventive, they can also become overly preoccupied with their own thoughts and socially awkward. At their best, thinkers are trailblazing visionaries.

6

THE LOYALIST
The committed, traditionalist type. Responsible and reliable, loyalists can also be too partisan and unquestioning of authority. Usually endearing, they can become defensive, evasive, and anxious. At their best, loyalists are stable and brave supporters of the weak.

7

THE GENERALIST
The enthusiastic, productive type. Generalists are outgoing and optimistic, full of spontaneity and high spirits. Although accomplished, they run the risk of becoming undisciplined and overextended. At their best, generalists focus their talents joyously.

8

THE LEADER
The powerful, aggressive type. Leaders are strong, assertive, and resourceful. Protective and decisive, they can also be bossy and intimidating. At their worst, they are openly unjust and belligerent. At their best, leaders become heroes, using their strength to improve others' lives.

The paired statements at right are part of a test used to determine personality type according to the Enneagram. A person chooses which statement in each pair better describes how he or she feels and behaves most of the time; the choice reflects a preference for one of the nine types over another. (Links between statements and types are not revealed during the test.) The type selected most often over 144 such pairs indicates the individual's basic personality type.

ARTIST OR THINKER?
1. One of my greatest assets is the depth of my feelings.
2. One of my greatest assets is the sharpness of my mind.

LEADER OR PEACEMAKER?
1. Although I know how to relax, I am basically hard-driving.
2. Although I can be ambitious, I am basically easygoing.

HELPER OR GENERALIST?
1. I tend to be sympathetic and accept what people tell me about themselves.
2. I tend to be skeptical and don't believe every story I hear.

PEACEMAKER OR REFORMER?
1. Why focus on the negative when there is so much that's wonderful about life?
2. I don't like being critical, but I can't help noticing when things are wrong.

The chart at right lists descriptions of the 16 personality types identified by the Myers-Briggs Type Indicator. Types are grouped according to preferences for either extraversion (E) or introversion (I), sensing (S) or intuition (N), thinking (T) or feeling (F), and judging (J) or perceiving (P). The descriptions reflect the Myers-Briggs philosophy that every type has its own merits and that no single personality is better than another. Myers hoped to help people be more accepting of themselves and more appreciative of what makes others different.

UNDERSTANDING OTHERS AND OURSELVES

Carl Jung's pioneering work on psychological types has inspired its share of admirers over the years. Perhaps none was more ardent than Katharine Briggs, a self-taught student of personality who elaborated on Jung's insights. Briggs's daughter, Isabel Myers, in turn enlarged on her mother's ideas and, in the 1950s and 1960s, devised a classification scheme known as the Myers-Briggs Type Indicator (MBTI). Her goal was to encourage an appreciation of the fundamental differences between people.

The MBTI categorizes individuals on the basis of four dichotomies. First, each of us is thought to prefer one of two distinct ways of perceiving the world: directly through the senses or more abstractly, drawing on intuitive processes. Each person also is assumed to prefer one of two ways of making judgments, by thinking or by feeling. Thinking involves a logical pursuit of objective decisions. Feeling aims at determining value according to more-subjective criteria.

In turn, perceptions and judgments are influenced by whether a person is chiefly interested in the inner world of concepts and ideas, or the outer world of people and objects—a difference to which Jung gave the labels introversion and extraversion. Finally, each of us tends to rely on perception more than judgment or vice versa. Different combinations of these aspects account for the MBTI's 16 personality types.

		SENSING		INTUITIVE	
		THINKING	FEELING	FEELING	THINKING
INTROVERTS	JUDGING	**ISTJ** Serious, quiet, earn success by concentration and thoroughness. Practical, orderly, matter-of-fact, logical, realistic, and dependable. See to it that everything is well organized. Take responsibility. Make up their own mind as to what should be accomplished and work toward it steadily, regardless of protests or distractions.	**ISFJ** Quiet, friendly, responsible, and conscientious. Work devotedly to meet their obligations. Lend stability to any project or group. Thorough, painstaking, accurate. Their interests are usually not technical. Can be patient with necessary details. Loyal, considerate, perceptive, concerned with how other people feel.	**INFJ** Succeed by perseverance, originality, and desire to do whatever is needed or wanted. Put their best efforts into their work. Quietly forceful, conscientious, concerned for others. Respected for their firm principles. Likely to be honored and followed for their clear convictions as to how best to serve the common good.	**INTJ** Usually have original minds and great drive for their own ideas and purposes. In fields that appeal to them, they have a fine power to organize a job and carry it through with or without help. Skeptical, critical, independent, determined, sometimes stubborn. Must learn to yield less-important points in order to win the most important.
INTROVERTS	PERCEIVING	**ISTP** Cool onlookers—quiet, reserved, observing and analyzing life with detached curiosity and unexpected flashes of original humor. Usually interested in cause and effect, how and why mechanical things work, and in organizing facts using logical principles.	**ISFP** Retiring, quietly friendly, sensitive, kind, modest about their abilities. Shun disagreements, do not force their opinions or values on others. Usually do not care to lead but are often loyal followers. Often relaxed about getting things done, because they enjoy the present moment and do not want to spoil it by undue haste or exertion.	**INFP** Full of enthusiasms and loyalties, but seldom talk of these until they know you well. Care about learning, ideas, language, and independent projects of their own. Tend to undertake too much, then somehow get it done. Friendly, but often too absorbed in what they are doing to be sociable. Little concerned with possessions or physical surroundings.	**INTP** Quiet and reserved. Especially enjoy theoretical or scientific pursuits. Like solving problems with logic and analysis. Usually interested mainly in ideas, with little liking for parties or small talk. Tend to have sharply defined interests. Need careers where some strong interest can be used and is useful.
EXTRAVERTS	PERCEIVING	**ESTP** Good at on-the-spot problem solving. Do not worry, enjoy whatever comes along. Tend to like mechanical things and sports, with friends on the side. Adaptable, tolerant, generally conservative in values. Dislike long explanations. Are best with real things that can be worked, handled, taken apart, or put together.	**ESFP** Outgoing, easygoing, accepting, friendly, enjoy everything and make things more fun for others by their enjoyment. Like sports and making things happen. Know what's going on and join in eagerly. Find remembering facts easier than mastering theories. Are best in situations that need common sense and practical ability with people as well as things.	**ENFP** Warmly enthusiastic, high-spirited, ingenious, imaginative. Able to do almost anything that interests them. Quick with a solution for any difficulty and ready to help anyone with a problem. Often rely on their ability to improvise instead of preparing in advance. Can usually find compelling reasons for whatever they want.	**ENTP** Quick, ingenious, good at many things. Stimulating company, alert and outspoken. May argue for fun on either side of a question. Resourceful in solving new and challenging problems, but may neglect routine assignments. Apt to turn to one new interest after another. Skillful in finding logical reasons for what they want.
EXTRAVERTS	JUDGING	**ESTJ** Practical, realistic, matter-of-fact, with a natural head for business or mechanics. Not interested in subjects they see no use for, but can apply themselves when necessary. Like to organize and run activities. May make good administrators, especially if they remember to consider others' feelings and points of view.	**ESFJ** Warm-hearted, talkative, popular, conscientious, born cooperators, active committee members. Need harmony and may be good at creating it. Always doing something nice for someone. Work best with encouragement and praise. Main interest in things that directly and visibly affect people's lives.	**ENFJ** Responsive and responsible. Generally feel real concern for what others think or want, and try to handle things with due regard for the other person's feelings. Can present a proposal or lead a group discussion with ease and tact. Sociable, popular, sympathetic. Responsive to praise and criticism.	**ENTJ** Hearty, frank, decisive, leaders in activities. Usually good in anything that requires reasoning and intelligent talk, such as public speaking. Are usually well informed and enjoy adding to their fund of knowledge. May sometimes appear more positive and confident than their experience in an area warrants.

The questions at right are from a popular version of the Myers-Briggs test used to evaluate personality. Each question pertains to one of the four aspects of personality and assesses which of that aspect's two alternatives the respondent prefers. (As with the Enneagram, the Myers-Briggs test does not indicate which aspect a particular question addresses so that answers will be unbiased.) Scores for more than 100 questions determine the respondent's type.

EXTRAVERT OR INTROVERT?
At parties, do you
(A) stay late, with increasing energy?
(B) leave early, with decreased energy?

SENSING OR INTUITIVE?
In doing ordinary things, are you more likely to
(A) do it the usual way?
(B) do it your own way?

THINKING OR FEELING?
In judging others, are you more swayed by
(A) laws than circumstances?
(B) circumstances than laws?

JUDGING OR PERCEIVING?
Are you more comfortable
(A) after a decision?
(B) before a decision?

Costa and McCrae's system of personality evaluation, known as the NEO-PI (Neuroticism-Extraversion-Openness Personality Inventory), rates individuals in the five general domains listed at right. Which of three descriptions for each domain best fits a given person depends on responses to a series of statements *(bottom right)* that represent each domain's defining characteristics. High scores reflect agreement with statements and thus a tendency to exhibit the traits of the corresponding domain.

THE FIVE DOMAINS OF PERSONALITY

While approaches such as the Enneagram and the Myers-Briggs test focus on determining an individual's distinct type, other methods place more emphasis on the traits from which personality takes shape. One such example, devised beginning in the 1970s by researchers Paul T. Costa Jr. and Robert R. McCrae, identifies five groups of related traits known as domains: neuroticism, extraversion, openness, agreeableness, and conscientiousness. The varying degrees to which people manifest these traits or their opposites provide a less-absolute definition of character.

Neuroticism refers to a proneness—or lack thereof—to disturbing emotions, including anxiety, hostility, depression, self-consciousness, impulsiveness, and vulnerability. Extraversion is characterized much the same as in other systems. Openness relates to a person's receptiveness to new ideas and experiences. Subjects evaluate how open-minded they are about such concepts as fantasy, aesthetics, feelings, and values.

Agreeableness can be seen in selfless concern for others and in generous impulses; its component traits include trust, straightforwardness, altruism, compliance, modesty, and a sympathetic attitude toward others. Finally, conscientiousness applies to what was once referred to simply as "character." A high rating in this domain suggests the presence of such traits as dutifulness, self-discipline, and deliberation.

	HIGH SCORE	NEUTRAL SCORE	LOW SCORE
NEUROTICISM	Sensitive, emotional, and prone to experience feelings that are upsetting.	Generally calm and able to deal with stress, but you sometimes experience feelings of guilt, anger, or sadness.	Secure, hardy, and generally relaxed even under stressful conditions.
EXTRAVERSION	Extraverted, outgoing, active, and high-spirited. You prefer to be around people most of the time.	Moderate in activity and enthusiasm. You enjoy the company of others but also value privacy.	Introverted, reserved, and serious. You prefer to be alone or with a few close friends.
OPENNESS	Open to new experiences. You have broad interests, and you are very imaginative.	Practical but willing to consider new ways of doing things. You seek a balance between the old and the new.	Down-to-earth, practical, traditional, and pretty much set in your ways.
AGREEABLENESS	Compassionate, good-natured, and eager to cooperate and avoid conflict.	Generally warm, trusting, and agreeable, but you can sometimes be stubborn and competitive.	Hardheaded, skeptical, proud, and competitive. You tend to express your anger directly.
CONSCIENTIOUSNESS	Conscientious and well organized. You have high standards and always strive to achieve your goals.	Dependable and moderately well organized. You generally have clear goals but are able to set your work aside.	Easygoing, not very well organized, and sometimes careless. You prefer not to make plans.

The NEO-PI test consists of 240 first-person statements, each related to one of the five personality domains. Individuals rate their agreement with each statement on a scale from 1 to 5, from strong disagreement to strong agreement. Another version of the test phrases similar statements in the third person and is intended for more-objective evaluations by peers, spouses, or professionals.

NEUROTICISM
I rarely feel fearful or anxious.

EXTRAVERSION
I don't get much pleasure from chatting with people.

OPENNESS
I don't like to waste my time daydreaming.

AGREEABLENESS
I tend to assume the best about people.

CONSCIENTIOUSNESS
I pride myself on my sound judgment.

THE PHYSICAL ROOTS OF WHO WE ARE

Ever since researchers first began investigating the fascinating puzzle of human behavior, a debate has raged as to whether biology or environment—nature or nurture—plays the greater role in the formation of personality. Recent studies offer some support to the notion that genes are responsible not only for physical traits but for psychological ones as well. Still, the argument remains far from settled, in part because of the many subtle influences at work.

To begin with, human biology is so intricate that identifying the specific physiological underpinnings of a given behavior—which likely involve several of the brain's myriad chemical processes—always poses a major challenge. In turn, what we call personality typically consists of a complex combination of traits, making it that much harder to determine just which genes may be responsible for which aspects of behavior. And defining where genetic effects end and environmental influences begin may be the most difficult task of all.

Nonetheless, as described on the following pages, scientists have traced some of personality's biological underpinnings—confirming in the process that the genetic legacy carried by sperm (*right*) and egg helps shape psyche as well as physique.

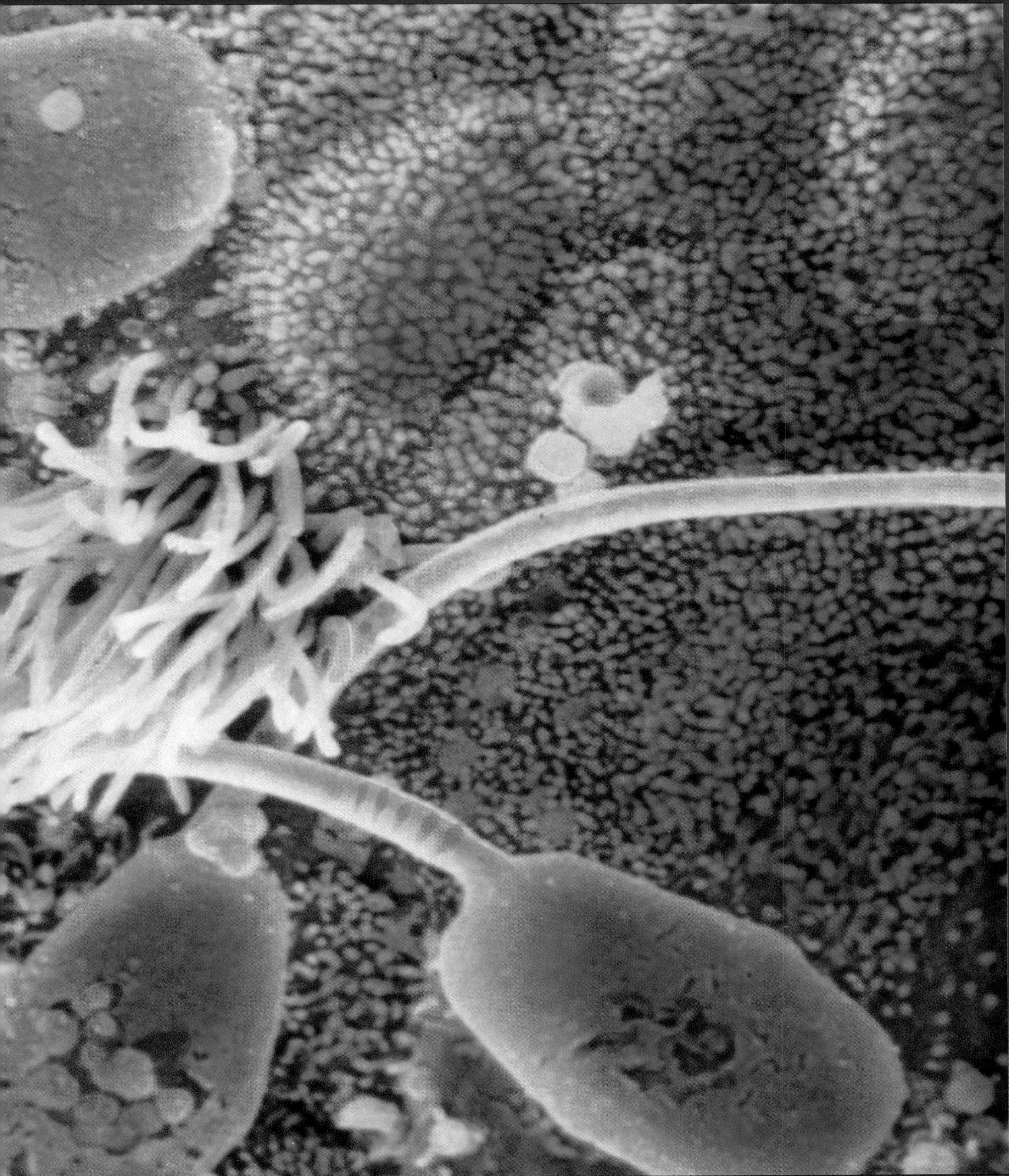

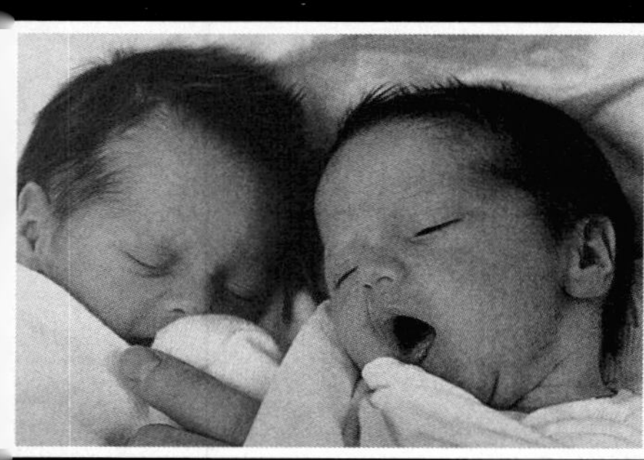

TWIN BODIES, TWIN SELVES?

The strongest evidence that personality has a hereditary basis comes from studies comparing twins. Identical twins, which result from the splitting of an egg after it has been fertilized, have precisely the same genetic makeup, so any differences between them would have to owe to environmental influences. Conversely, psychological similarities between identical twins who have been raised apart—and thus subject to different environments—presumably must stem from their shared heredity. By examining such cases of separated twins, researchers have discovered just how influential genes can be.

In studies measuring specific personality traits such as extraversion, identical twins match up much more often than fraternal twins, who provide a useful contrast because they are genetically no more alike than any other siblings. The results for twins separated at birth have been much the same, with a greater correlation between identical than between fraternal twins. Indeed, many investigators conclude that variations in the family environment have little effect on inherent aspects of personality.

Genes, of course, make their influence felt by determining such biological features as the structure of the brain and the way it handles the many chemicals that make it tick. As a result, researchers have increasingly turned their focus on how physiology itself shapes personality.

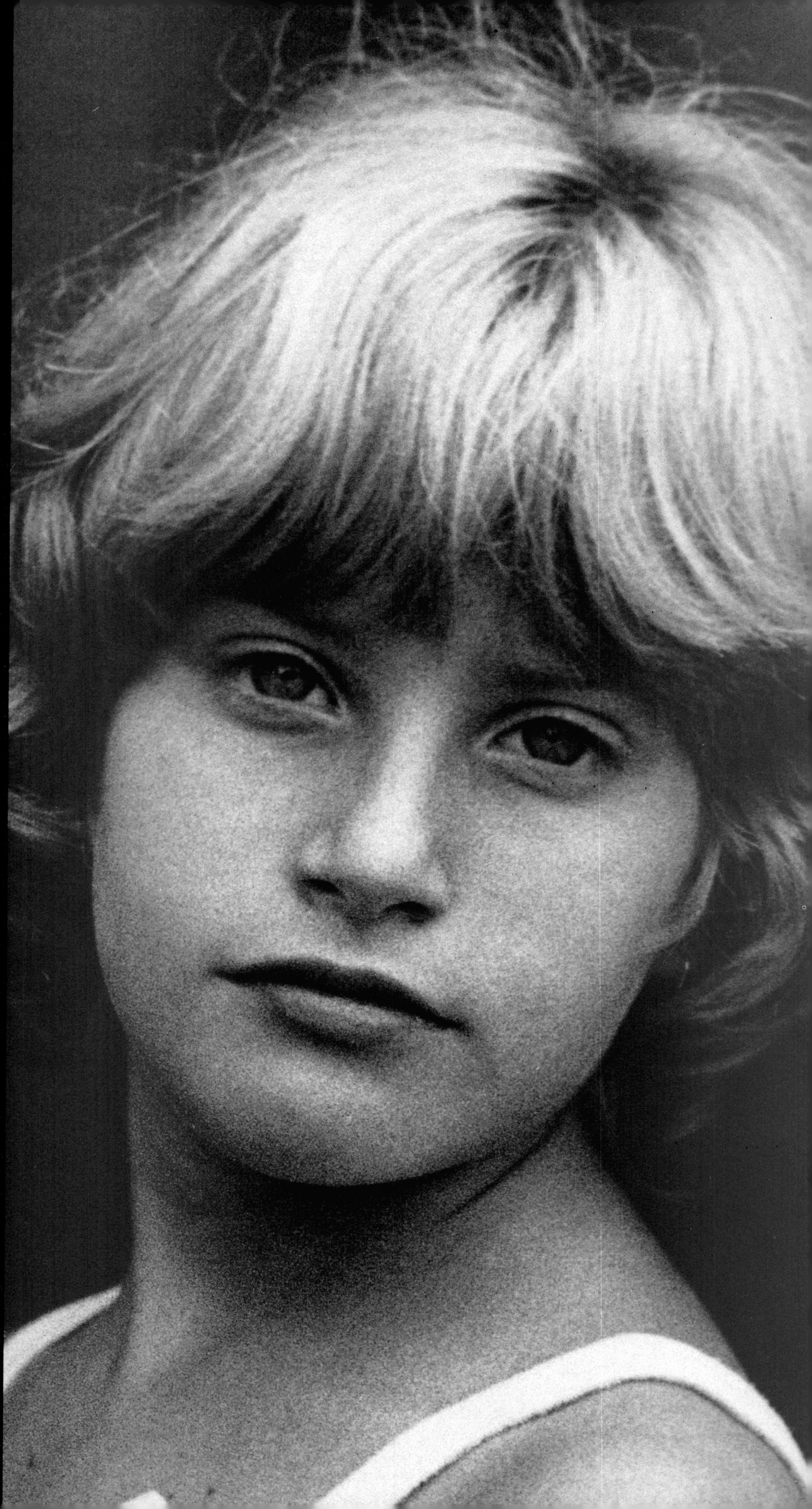

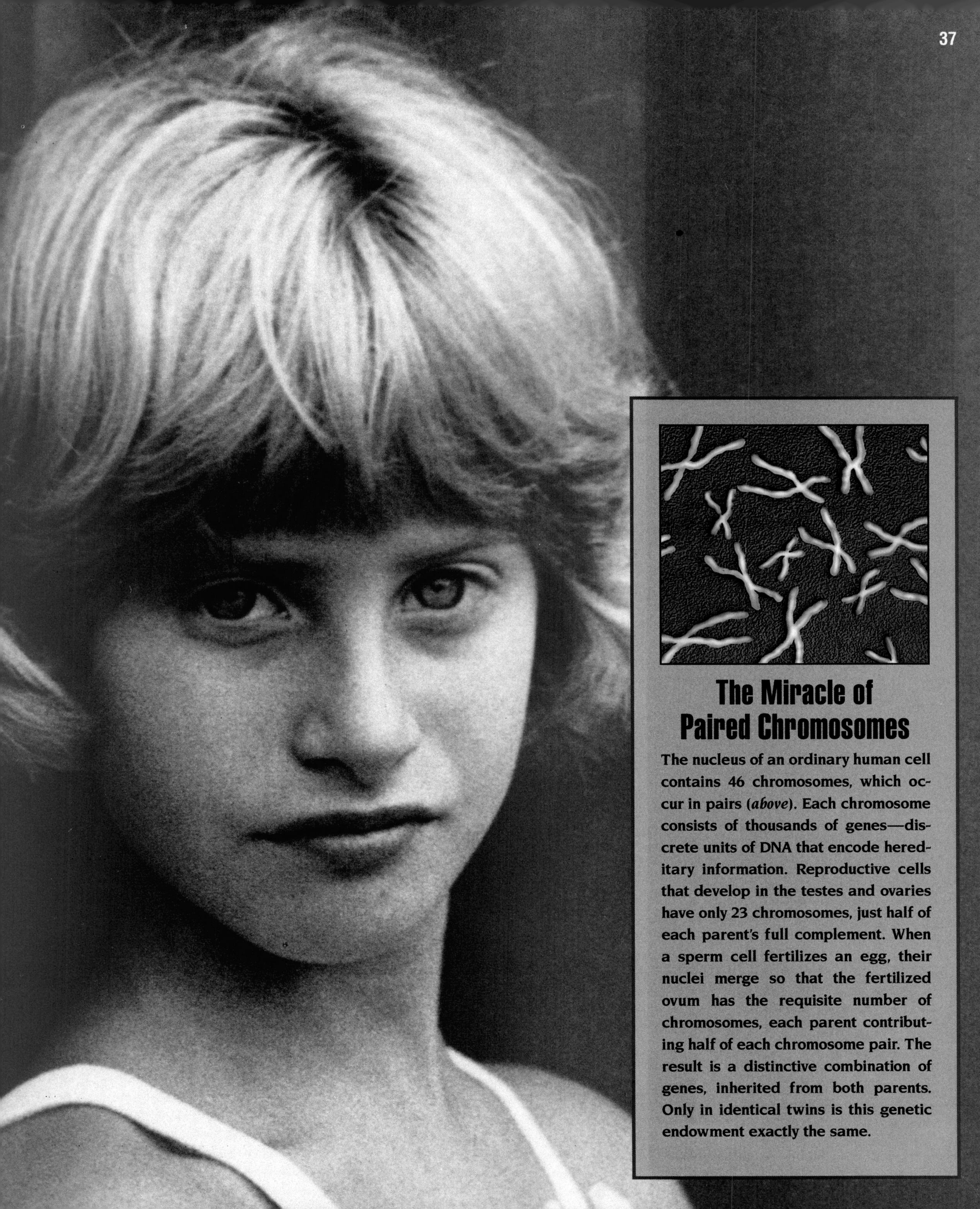

The Miracle of Paired Chromosomes

The nucleus of an ordinary human cell contains 46 chromosomes, which occur in pairs (*above*). Each chromosome consists of thousands of genes—discrete units of DNA that encode hereditary information. Reproductive cells that develop in the testes and ovaries have only 23 chromosomes, just half of each parent's full complement. When a sperm cell fertilizes an egg, their nuclei merge so that the fertilized ovum has the requisite number of chromosomes, each parent contributing half of each chromosome pair. The result is a distinctive combination of genes, inherited from both parents. Only in identical twins is this genetic endowment exactly the same.

BEHAVIOR AND THE AROUSED BRAIN

One of the clearest indications that personality has physiological roots involves the traits known as introversion and extraversion, which seem to be related to variations in the arousal of specific parts of the brain. According to a theory proposed by Hans Eysenck (*pages* 19-20), the fundamental difference between these two traits originates in the limbic system, which plays a major role in emotion and instinctive behavior. A central element of the limbic system is the reticular formation in the brainstem, which receives sensory input and passes it on to the cerebrum, where the data are processed and interpreted. The majority of this processing is handled by the outer layer of the cerebrum, known as the cerebral cortex, which controls such complex aspects of behavior as thought and planning.

Eysenck's theory posits that, for the reticular formation and thus the cortex, there is an optimum level of inherent arousal, or stimulation—separate from any external sensory stimulation. In extraverts, according to Eysenck, that optimum level is not met, while in introverts it is exceeded. The two types behave differently, says Eysenck, in an unconscious effort to reach the proper threshold: Extraverts seek extra stimulation to increase the level of sensory input and thus arousal; introverts avoid stimulation or engage in repetitive behaviors that, through habituation, help lower inherent arousal.

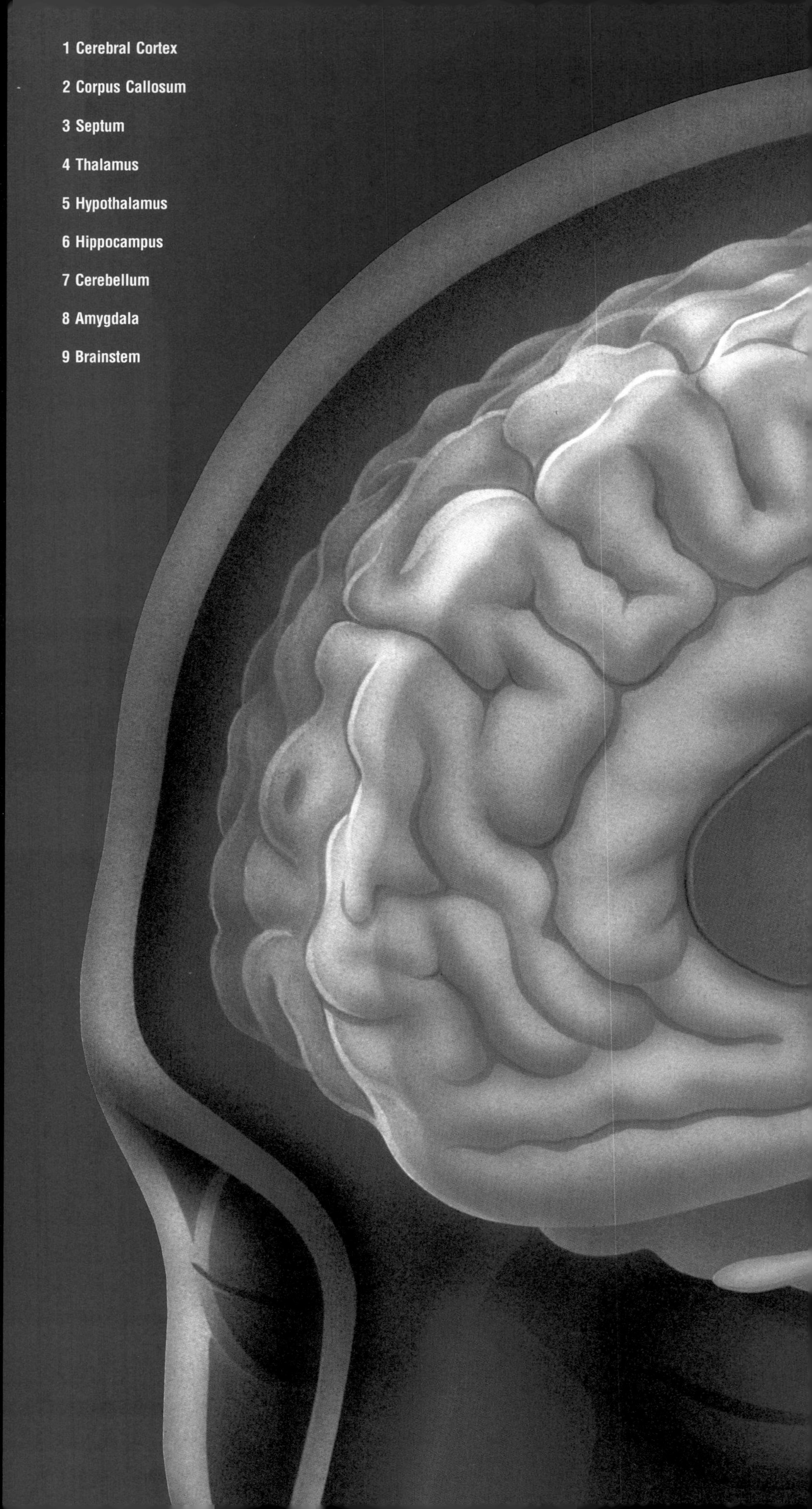

1 Cerebral Cortex
2 Corpus Callosum
3 Septum
4 Thalamus
5 Hypothalamus
6 Hippocampus
7 Cerebellum
8 Amygdala
9 Brainstem

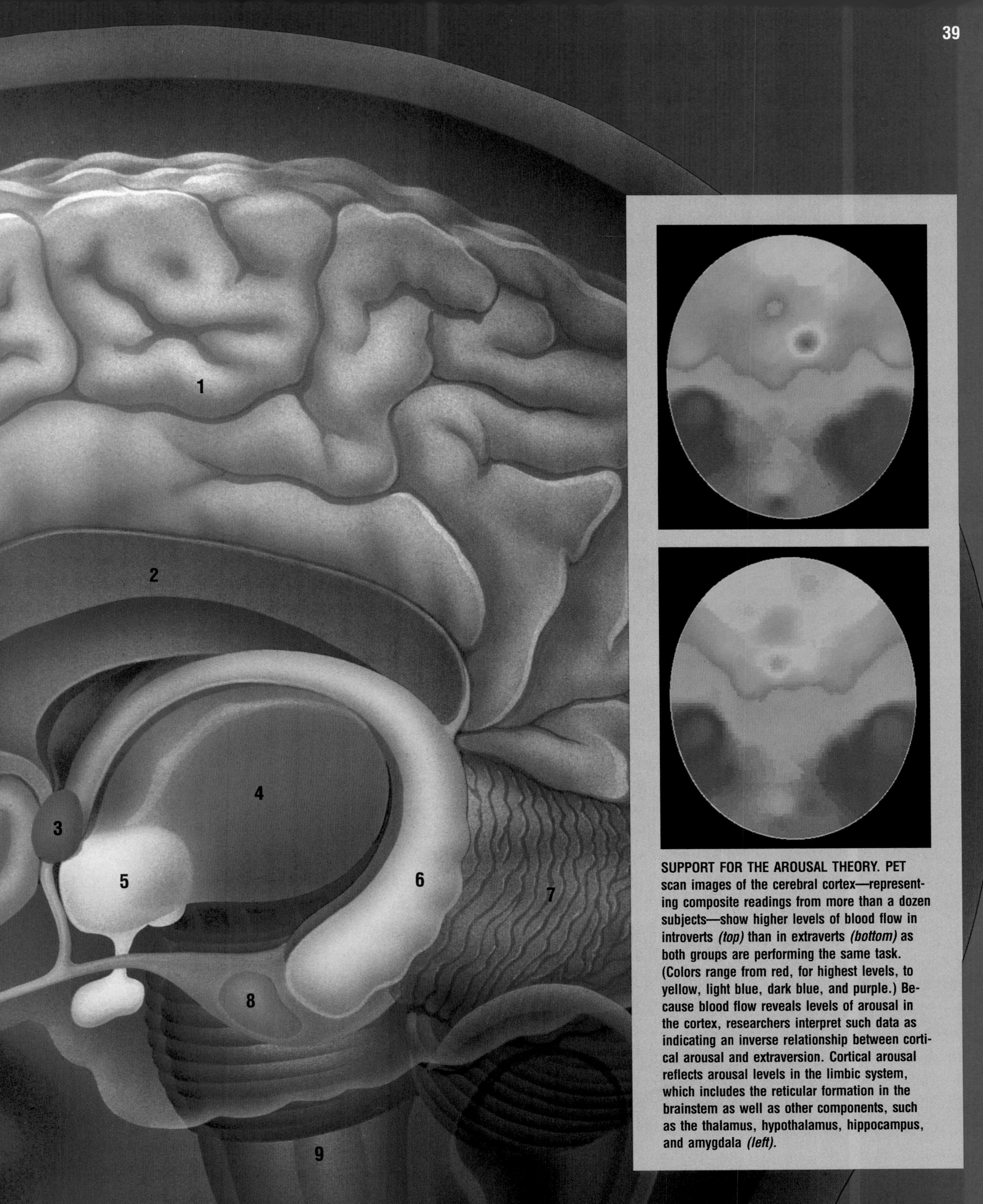

SUPPORT FOR THE AROUSAL THEORY. PET scan images of the cerebral cortex—representing composite readings from more than a dozen subjects—show higher levels of blood flow in introverts *(top)* than in extraverts *(bottom)* as both groups are performing the same task. (Colors range from red, for highest levels, to yellow, light blue, dark blue, and purple.) Because blood flow reveals levels of arousal in the cortex, researchers interpret such data as indicating an inverse relationship between cortical arousal and extraversion. Cortical arousal reflects arousal levels in the limbic system, which includes the reticular formation in the brainstem as well as other components, such as the thalamus, hypothalamus, hippocampus, and amygdala *(left)*.

AN INHERENT YEN FOR SENSATION

Another behavioral trait that may be influenced by brain physiology is sensation seeking, which is characterized by a need for new and varied experiences along with the acceptance of physical and social risks to get them. This quality appears to be associated with the relative abundance of certain neurotransmitters, the vital chemicals that carry signals between the neurons of the brain.

The neurotransmitters involved in sensation seeking are dopamine, which has been implicated in aggression and sexual behavior, and norepinephrine, which increases brain activity and helps keep the body primed for action. The brain sometimes converts dopamine into norepinephrine.

The body controls neurotransmitter levels by balancing their production and destruction. A key player in dopamine destruction is the enzyme monoamine oxidase (MAO). Low MAO levels result in higher levels of dopamine, and thus presumably of norepinephrine. The behavioral effects have been shown in animal studies: In a colony of monkeys, the more dominant, playful, and aggressive individuals tended to have low MAO levels.

Humans who rank high in sensation seeking also tend to have low MAO levels. Further evidence of a connection between the enzyme and the behavior is the fact that sensation seeking declines with age—corresponding to increased MAO levels observed in older people.

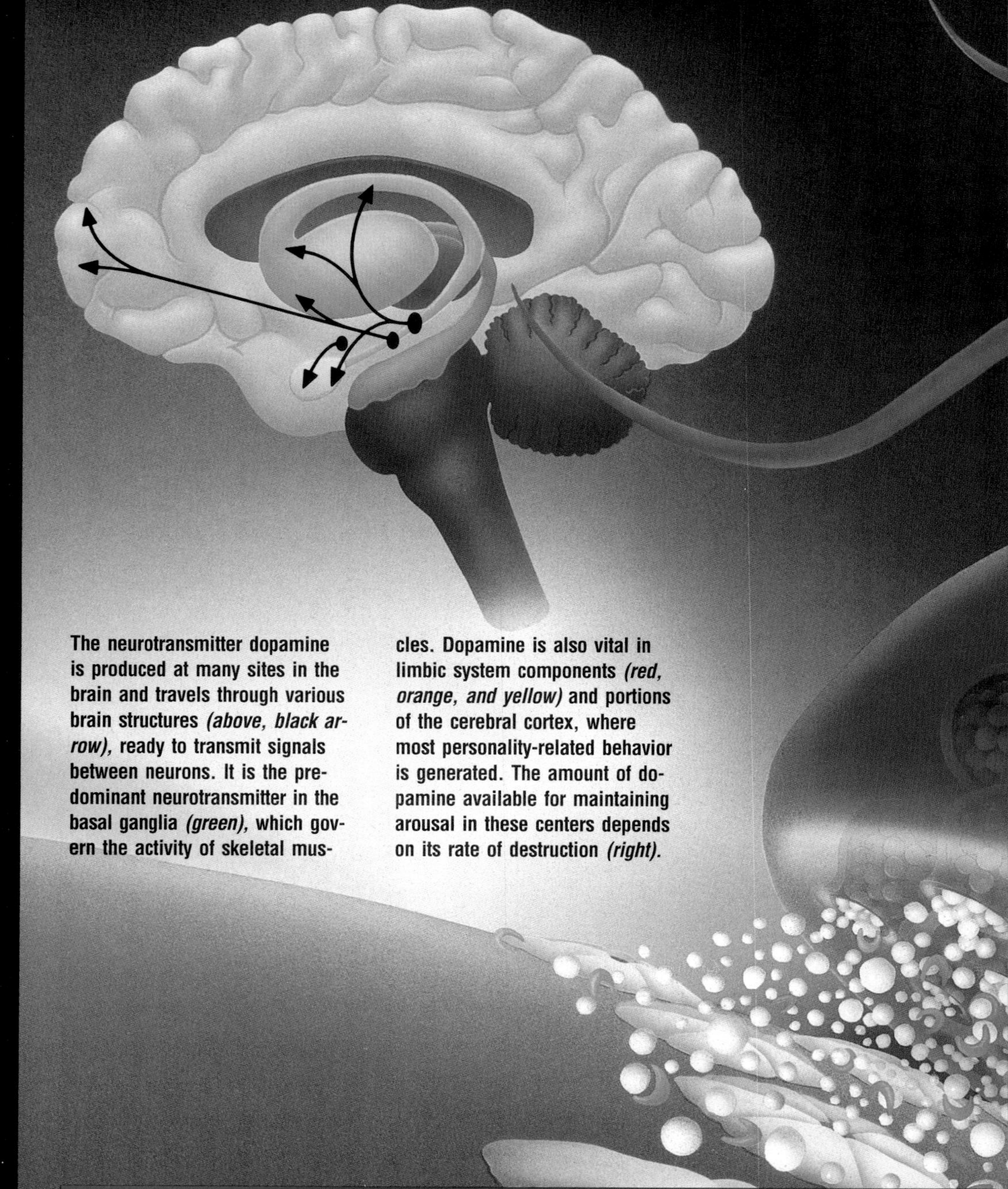

The neurotransmitter dopamine is produced at many sites in the brain and travels through various brain structures *(above, black arrow),* ready to transmit signals between neurons. It is the predominant neurotransmitter in the basal ganglia *(green),* which govern the activity of skeletal muscles. Dopamine is also vital in limbic system components *(red, orange, and yellow)* and portions of the cerebral cortex, where most personality-related behavior is generated. The amount of dopamine available for maintaining arousal in these centers depends on its rate of destruction *(right).*

Sex, Hormones, and Seeking Thrills

The fact that men seem more prone than women to sensation seeking has led researchers to focus on what effect sex hormones may have on this trait. Studies indicate that males scoring high on measures of sensation seeking tend to have higher blood levels of the male hormone testosterone than those with low scores. The process by which testosterone affects sensation seeking apparently involves the enzyme MAO: Testosterone has been shown to inhibit its production.

The female hormone estrogen also reduces MAO levels. Unlike testosterone, however, estrogen is not produced at a constant rate: Levels fluctuate during the menstrual cycle, leading some researchers to speculate that estrogen's effects on MAO may account for some of the mood changes associated with the cycle.

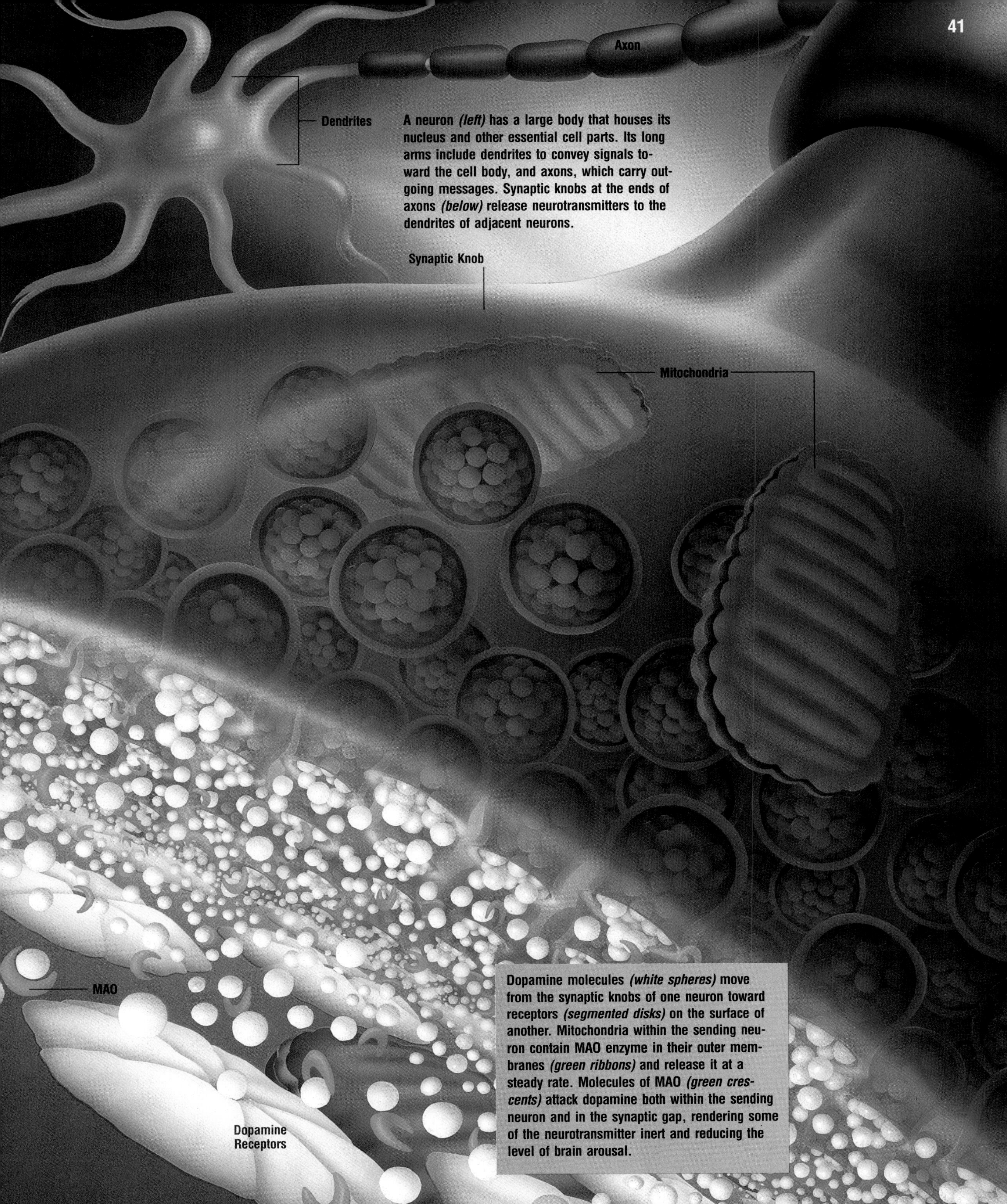

A neuron *(left)* has a large body that houses its nucleus and other essential cell parts. Its long arms include dendrites to convey signals toward the cell body, and axons, which carry outgoing messages. Synaptic knobs at the ends of axons *(below)* release neurotransmitters to the dendrites of adjacent neurons.

Dopamine molecules *(white spheres)* move from the synaptic knobs of one neuron toward receptors *(segmented disks)* on the surface of another. Mitochondria within the sending neuron contain MAO enzyme in their outer membranes *(green ribbons)* and release it at a steady rate. Molecules of MAO *(green crescents)* attack dopamine both within the sending neuron and in the synaptic gap, rendering some of the neurotransmitter inert and reducing the level of brain arousal.

2

Recipe for an Individual

Few experiences inspire a sense of human oneness quite so vividly as a visit to a maternity ward. There, dreaming unknown dreams behind delicate eyelids, are the latest additions to the human family, the heirs and perpetuators of what we are as a species. Viewed in their newness, all swaddled in soft blankets and wearing knitted caps to keep their heads warm, the little residents of the ward—virtually indistinguishable, perhaps even to their own parents—give the impression of generic babyhood. Yet every one of the infants is unique, and not just in such physical traits as eye color, hair texture, and ear size, but also in behavior.

Some of their behavioral distinctiveness becomes evident even before they enter the world. One baby may lie quietly in the womb waiting to be born, while another may give the mother hardly a moment's rest, kicking and bicycling all the way through the final months of pregnancy. At birth, an infant may emit hardly a peep; after drawing in that first breath, he or she may spend an hour quietly taking in the surroundings. Another may squall loudly and then, after a few minutes, fall into a deep sleep. At feeding, one infant may suck eagerly and sloppily, while another becomes finicky, requiring a great deal of coaxing before settling

The Shaping of Character before the First Breath

Many studies point to factors that affect the physical development of a fetus, with a particular focus on the disastrous consequences of alcohol or drug use or maternal illness. But some investigators suspect that the mother's emotional and psychological state may influence not only the fetus's physical well-being but the formation of personality as well.

The fetus whose mother is calm and relaxed inhabits a much different environment from the one whose mother is anxious or tense. One sign of the difference is that women who report being emotionally distraught during pregnancy seem to have more physically active fetuses. Although researchers remain unsure of the implications of this heightened activity for fetal development, they have found a demonstrable connection between anxiety and occurrences of nausea during pregnancy, premature birth, prolonged labor, and higher use of anesthesia during delivery. As a result, anxious mothers are more likely to give birth to children with physical problems.

Even healthy newborns whose mothers were unusually anxious apparently suffer ill effects. Examinations of such infants conducted soon after birth reveal them to be hyperactive and irritable. They cry more than children who have experienced an uneventful birthing process and are more likely to have feeding and sleeping difficulties—conditions that have been linked to distinct personality types manifested later in life.

down to the breast or the bottle. Some babies are extremely alert, jumping at an unexpected sound or sight. Others seem relatively oblivious to the noises around them. Some cry frequently and work themselves into furious tantrums; others quickly become used to a regular schedule of eating and sleeping, causing their parents hardly a moment's annoyance. All such traits and temperaments warrant the word *normal*, meaning that they fall within the behavioral spectrum that physicians and psychologists consider the normal range.

Fundamentally, the behavioral makeup of a newborn is scripted by genes, the miraculously concentrated molecular instructions that prescribe how humans and all other organisms take form. But a baby's genes are only part of the story. Like physical development, the development of behavior results from the interaction of genes and the environment. (In the behavioral sciences, the term *environment* covers not just such factors as upbringing and social surroundings but also such nonhereditary biological factors as nutrition, accidents, or illness.) Most of the time, the dynamic partnership goes well, but not always. The interplay of genetic and environmental factors can lead to developmental distortions at any time, including during the protected period of gestation. For example, the use of alcohol or cocaine by the mother during pregnancy may cause lasting psychological problems in her child, and a maternal diet lacking proper nutrition and vitamins may prevent the child from ever achieving the IQ level that otherwise might have been reached.

Compared to what comes later, the womb is a highly stable environment. After birth, whatever behavioral tendencies the child has brought into the world will be subjected to a huge array of environmental influences—culture, parents, siblings, socioeconomic

ORIGINS OF ATTACHMENT. In a series of experiments with infant monkeys in the late 1960s, University of Wisconsin professor Harry Harlow gained new insights into the phenomenon known as attachment—the bond formed between infant and mother in the earliest stages of life. Attachment was initially thought to result from the child's dependence on the mother for nourishment, but Harlow found otherwise. As shown at right, rhesus monkeys would consistently cling to a surrogate mother covered in terry cloth even when they were fed by a less-realistic wire-mesh monkey outfitted with a bottle. Harlow also observed a common behavior known as stranger anxiety. When confronted with a fear-provoking buglike object *(below)*, the infant monkeys ran to the terry cloth mother for comfort—then later, apparently encouraged by their "mother's" presence, ventured out to examine the novel stimulus.

factors, relationships with peers and teachers, plus a potentially infinite variety of life experiences. No two individuals, even within the same family, will ever be exposed to exactly the same environment. As a result, every human being, even a twin or triplet who has a genetically identical sibling, is a unique individual.

Although behavior's basic developmental formula of interaction between genes and the environment is clear enough, many of the details are not. The field of behavioral development, never a sedate precinct of the sciences, remains rich in questions, mysteries, and controversies. At the same time, there is a strong sense of progress in the air, of forward movement on many fronts. Research has been mostly unkind to the old picture of a child as almost infinitely malleable—a tabula rasa, or blank slate, in the phrase of the 17th-century philosopher John Locke. Not only is it clear that children are born with distinct personality traits, but there is also growing statistical proof that some of those traits persist throughout life; they appear to be more deeply etched than once was thought.

Conventional wisdom has also been challenged by studies documenting that child-parent interactions are very much a two-way street: The child, it now appears, may play an important role in shaping his or her environment. Studies of identical twins have produced some of the most provocative findings of all, indicating, for instance, that parents' general approach to child raising has a more limited effect than most psychologists and social scientists assumed. Added to all of these insights and revisions is an ever-growing body of descriptive information about personality—data on how it may affect school performance in early childhood, self-confidence in adolescence, and the choice of mate and career in adulthood.

Even as knowledge of the workings of personality accumulates, some researchers are continuing the grandly scaled endeavor launched by Sigmund Freud—the quest for overall patterns in the development of human behavior. As with Freud's notions of a series of psychosexual transitions (passage through "oral," "anal," and "phallic" periods by the age of five, for example) most such big-picture theories describe a sequence of stages of development, a kind of inexorable unfolding that is standardized for the species.

Among the most influential of 20th-century developmental theorists—and certainly one of the most original—was a Swiss psychologist named Jean Piaget. Born in 1896, Piaget knew little of the usual joys of childhood: His mother was exceedingly pious and emotionally unstable, and his father, a history professor, was stern and remote. Perhaps in consequence, Piaget chose to focus on children when he took up a scientific career. His particular interest was cognitive development, the growth of mental powers from birth to adolescence.

Piaget was a superbly gifted observer. Indeed, he revolutionized psychology by interacting directly with children, playing games with them and asking detailed questions about their dreams, their fantasies, and their fears. In one exercise, for example, he would place his hat on a toy to see whether a child realized that the object was under the hat; he found that, up to the age of nine months, most children were unaware that the toy lay hidden there. Older children, having progressed to a later stage of cognitive development, showed by their reactions that they understood the trick.

On the basis of hundreds of such experiments carried out over a period of six decades, Piaget postulated a series of four major developmental stages through which children advance on their way to adulthood.

In the first stage—called sensorimotor and lasting from birth until about the age of two—the child learns to deal with external objects through the senses and muscles. In the second stage—termed preoperational and continuing to the age of about seven—the child learns to talk about the world beyond the immediate ken of the senses but has an imperfect understanding of causality, time, quantity, and other organizing concepts. During the third stage—labeled concrete operations and extending to the age of about 12—the child learns how to think about relationships and becomes competent at such tasks as counting and classifying. In the fourth and last stage, formal operations, the child becomes able to draw up hypotheses, deal with abstract mathematical relationships, weigh possibilities, and analyze social or philosophical issues such as justice or ethical values.

This cognitive scheme has been criticized in some of its details and broader contentions, but virtually all psychologists agree that it has helped to illuminate the process of maturing.

It is not the only stage theory to excite widespread interest, however. Even as Jean Piaget painstakingly worked out his idea, a very different developmental sequence was proposed by a man named Erik Erikson, a follower of Freud's.

Erikson was born of Danish parents in 1902. Although his father was Protestant, Erikson was raised almost from birth by his Jewish mother and stepfather, who educated him in the Jewish tradition. This dual heritage sensitized him to the tension that each person experiences in forging an identity. He was slow to choose a career, first thinking he would be an artist, then taking a teaching post at

FATHERS AND BABIES. Because mothers usually occupy center stage when it comes to child rearing, psychologists have typically assumed that they have a much greater influence on personality development than fathers do. But the father's contribution is far from insignificant. Research has shown that fathers help to provide a secure base that allows infants to explore new social situations without fear. In addition, children who form a close bond with both parents tend to be more socially responsive than those whose primary attachment is to the mother. In most cases, the father becomes a child's preferred playmate; he is more likely to provide physical stimulation in the form of harmless roughhousing and to engage in all sorts of games, traditional and unpredictably original. This recreational relationship will contribute to the child's cognitive development, especially as the games become more intellectually challenging.

a small progressive school in Vienna. There he met and became a student of Freud's youngest daughter, Anna, who was studying the psychology of children. Erikson received his degree in 1933, and when Adolf Hitler rose to power, he fled Germany and went to the United States, becoming Boston's first child psychologist.

Erikson's view—presented in lectures, technical papers, and popular books—was that, in order to become fully mature, every individual must struggle through a series of socially oriented developmental stages that represent barriers to be overcome. (He optimistically believed that most people succeed in surmounting these barriers, though some take longer than others at each stage.) During the first year of life, said Erikson, the infant balances trust and mistrust. A successful child gains confidence that his mother will not abandon him and develops a lasting belief that he will be able to achieve his needs and wants. Between ages one and three, a child enters another stage, balancing autonomy against shame or doubt, developing a sense of independent will while overcoming anxiety about venturing away from mother.

Children between three and six, ac-

The Lasting Effects of a Family Divided

Although some researchers challenge the notion that parents play a crucial role in determining a child's personality, there is little doubt that drastic disruptions in the family environment are capable of altering the course of personality development. In the case of divorce, the effects seem to be meted out somewhat unequally between the sexes.

For one thing, daughters tend to adjust more rapidly to new parenting arrangements than do sons. Because an overwhelming majority of single-parent households are headed by the mother, the short-term outcome of divorce may be a closer-than-usual mother-daughter relationship. In contrast, sons—who are left without a male role model, and in many cases a strong-willed disciplinarian, in the home—may become impulsive, aggressive, and antisocial.

Although daughters seem to have fewer immediate behavioral difficulties, some studies have revealed a delayed effect. Upon reaching adolescence, girls from divorced families may exhibit sexually precocious and inappropriately assertive behavior with male peers and adults.

Of course, not all children suffer such ill consequences. Many survive the turmoil of their parents' divorce with little sign of psychological scarring. These "survivors" apparently succeed by quickly adjusting to the new family dynamics, and they may even become stronger for having weathered the loss.

cording to Erikson, deal with initiative and guilt, learning to act without fear of punishment. Between six and 12 years of age, they balance industry and feelings of inferiority, focusing on attaining competence at chosen tasks, particularly schoolwork. In the years from 12 to 20, they face an "identity crisis"; the successful ones emerge with an enduring sense of their uniqueness as a person.

In young adulthood, from about 20 to 40 years of age, Erikson's theory held that people battle with intimacy versus isolation, aiming to achieve love and to share life with another person. In the next-to-last stage, from the ages of about 40 to 60, individuals balance an urge to create against a tendency to stagnate. And in the final stage, after the age of 65, they seek wisdom and satisfaction with life, balancing feelings of accomplishment against despair.

For many of Freud's followers, Erikson's division of life into these eight stages injected new vigor into psychoanalysis, and his work stimulated many subsequent studies. But, like Piaget's ideas, the eightfold path that Erikson charted became the target of a good deal of criticism. Among other things, he was faulted for not providing solid evidence to support his scheme. As psychologists have learned more about development, many of them have come to have doubts about certain aspects of both Piaget's and Erikson's stage theories. Although each of these two 20th-century giants accepted that behavior and personality are shaped by an interaction of genes and environment, they seemed to place too much emphasis on programmed behavior. Their stage theories appear to some psychologists to be excessively simplified biological templates—inborn patterns with a kind of sovereign developmental authority.

Despite concerns about the grand theories, investigators of behavior retain a lively interest in developmental patterns and pacing. Indeed, the pursuit of the facts has grown hotter than ever, and also more far-ranging. Some studies have explained developmental milestones unaccounted for by the great stage theorists. Moreover, research efforts have revealed many subtleties in the role of the environment in personality formation, lending detail and shading (and some altogether new perspectives) to earlier pictures of the process. For mainstream psychologists, the current view of behavioral development is something like this:

The bond between mother and baby is the primary relationship of early childhood, and children themselves play a part in establishing it. The process of attachment, as it is called, develops between the infant and the mother within the first few months. The baby helps form the bond by looking at the parent, smiling at her, and gurgling pleasantly. Children who form a warm, close bond with their mother in early life are thought to develop a strong sense of personal confidence that enables them to take risks. According to developmental psychologist Jerome Kagan of Harvard, they are also more likely to enjoy learning about the world around them and to obey the requests of their parents.

After children have formed an attachment, according to contemporary psychologists, they pass two key developmental mileposts. (The progression appears to be true for children of every culture, although the timing may differ.) One milepost is marked by an emotion called stranger anxiety—essentially a fear of a new and unfamiliar face, particularly when the child's mother is not present. It appears in American children sometime around the sixth month, peaks at eight months, and generally fades by the 15th month; children who grow up

in a rural setting, isolated from social contact, may exhibit this behavior for a longer period.

The second milepost is separation anxiety. It occurs when the child suddenly realizes that a parent has left the room, and it may trigger an outburst of weeping. This fear becomes evident at eight to 12 months in American children and fades at about two years of age. In time, the child begins to understand that strange faces are not necessarily threatening and that the parent will return.

During the first three or four years of life, children of all cultures learn how to interact with their parents, their brothers and sisters, and other children. In this socialization process, the child discovers for the first time that society prohibits certain behavior. For example, he or she discovers that it is not acceptable to urinate whenever and wherever the urge happens, but only in appropriate places. More important, children begin to learn about their own emotions and actions—and the consequences. They begin to show an awareness of right and wrong. In addition, by the age of about two, the child has begun to make clear distinctions between "mine" and "yours."

Psychologists have identified several areas of emotion and behavior that preoccupy children at this stage. One of the most important is aggression. Children playing with peers learn quickly that aggression—hitting another child to get a toy, for example—leads to retaliation. Even so, parents often note that their children finish nursery school more aggressive than they were going in because aggression is also often rewarded: Not only does the victim hand over the toy, but the teacher may also devote a great deal of attention to the troublemaker. In addition, excessive fussing and punishment can stimulate bullying behavior. The best method of damping aggression among preschoolers, some psychologists argue, is to reward cooperation instead. Despite these efforts, however, some aggressive children simply continue to be aggressive.

The same appears to be true of extreme dependency. By the age of three years, most children outgrow the need to be always close to mother, and by age five, American children are expected to dress themselves and play without supervision. But some overprotective parents may prolong the period of dependency, making it difficult for the child to develop a feeling of competence. The fear of strangers and strange situations, a developmentally important phase in the first two years, vanishes in the next two or three years and is replaced by

A GANG PERSONALITY? Anecdotal evidence has long suggested that adolescent gangs—such as the Los Angeles street gangs at left—serve as surrogate families, responsible for the socialization of their members. In the wake of increasing gang-related violence, more-intense examinations of gang behavior have added to the picture, revealing a specific group of personality traits consistently observed in gang members. This set of traits, forming what psychologists call the "defiant individualist character," includes intense competitiveness, a general mistrust of others, and self-reliance—attributes that are apparently fostered by the deprived socioeconomic conditions in which gangs flourish, as well as by the dynamics of the gang itself. Variations on this common theme have been linked to ethnic differences, but for the most part the pattern of personality remains remarkably the same.

a concern over imagined threats, such as ghosts and wild animals.

Specifics vary from one individual to another, but it is common for children at this age to have generalized fears of the unknown—a sign of their developing ability to think about intangible objects. These emotions may have a good effect, goading the child into action or creative play. But in an excessive form, they can be harmful. Some psychologists believe that parents may add to a child's anxiety by setting standards that seem impossible to meet. To avoid frustration, children may "regress" to more babyish behavior or blame others for things they have done.

The important process of "identification," in which the child picks out a model among older people to follow, also occurs at this time. Children tend to adopt someone of the same sex and general appearance to identify with, and their models may include teachers, other children at nursery school, a parent, or siblings. The absence of such a model can be debilitating. Several studies have shown—not surprisingly—that boys who lose a father early in life tend to have emotional problems. A high percentage of delinquent boys examined in one research project had lost a father during the preschool years.

When a child is ready to begin school at about the age of six, the development of personality and the process of self-definition within the peer group move into high gear. Personality traits that may have won the approval of mother and father may become less helpful. For example, the placid child, rewarded for quiet and obedient behavior up to this point, may now be at a disadvantage in a group situation. Suddenly the parents are not the sole praise givers, and sometimes they are not even the most important ones. As intellectual skills develop and school life demands more of a child's attention, teachers' approval may gain influence.

A child may have already undergone a sobering appraisal of self-worth before entering school—especially if he or she has older siblings—but nothing seems quite as important as the approval or disdain of peers. What makes classmates admire one girl and ignore another? The answer is not easy to discern. But psychologists have identified some qualities that seem to make a difference.

Physical features are important: Attractive children tend to be more popular, and with boys, size and strength are particularly respected. Aggressive and outgoing children seem to become leaders, while shy and self-deprecating children slip into the role of followers. Patterns that may last a lifetime are set in these early school years, researchers say, and it is here that the child's fundamental social response is established—some children becoming dominant, others submissive. Peer opinions influence not only social status but intellectual performance as well. If friends disparage schoolwork, the child may do the same.

Researchers see one clear change in the way school-age children conduct themselves in the classroom in contrast to preschoolers: They are much more conforming. The tendency to follow the leader is so strong at this age that children will knowingly give wrong answers to a question simply to stay in line with the first answer given.

Three pictures of Genie show
tion from a seemingly norma
months *(left)* to an adult alm
sonality on her 27th birthday
photograph below was taken
13½, shortly after she had co
tion of California authorities.

Wild Children

The years between infancy and the age of five, according to psychologists, are crucial to personality development. A child whose world somehow narrows to exclude, even for part of this time, the full range of childhood experience may well suffer personality difficulties later in life. In extreme cases of deprivation, the victims can barely speak and, having missed what linguists call the "critical period" of language acquisition, never learn to do so well. Without language, the coin of human thought, they are unable to reason. Utterly resistant to socialization, they must spend their days under close supervision or confined to an institution. In the lexicon of psychology, such a person is called a wild child.

One of the most pathetic cases ever documented is that of a California woman known only as Genie (*left*). Born in 1957 to an unassertive mother with failing eyesight and a father who often beat his wife, Genie had a reasonably normal life until the age of 20 months. At that time, her father came unhinged at the unexpected death of his own mother. Thereafter he confined Genie to a bedroom from which she would seldom emerge for the next 12 years.

Left alone in the curtained chamber and strapped naked to a potty-chair, Genie had no one to talk to or play with, no toys beyond an occasional empty cottage cheese container or thread spool. Her father, intolerant of sound, punished the girl severely for the slightest noise, suppressing her verbal urges. Some nights, he allowed her off the potty seat to lie down in a constraining sleeping bag of his own design.

Genie's plight became known in November 1970, after a vicious fight between her parents that frightened her mother into fleeing the house with Genie in tow. Workers at a family-aid office, noticing how awkwardly the 13½-year-old Genie shuffled along behind her mother, called the police, who took Genie away and charged both parents with child abuse.

Genie had the classic arrested personality of a wild child. She could neither speak nor think beyond the level of a little girl. Fed on baby food and cereal all her life, she had not learned to chew solid food, nor could she control her bowels or bladder. After five years' intensive instruction from a group of doctors and linguists, Genie learned rudimentary speech that improved her thinking abilities and allowed a few personality traits to emerge. Her doctors noted that she became outgoing—but in ways distorted by her unusually stunted language. She was, for example, unable to begin a conversation with someone who was not already looking at her. Genie's expedient solution to the problem was to grab her target's face and turn it toward her. Puberty brought out an intensely rebellious streak, which she expressed in part by going about unclothed and masturbating in public.

During the attempt at rehabilitation, Genie's mother visited regularly. (She had eluded jail on the abuse charges; the father had committed suicide years earlier.) In the mid-1980s, the woman sought and was granted guardianship of Genie, whom she moved to a home for mentally retarded adults. There Genie remains, a person so maltreated during her formative years that she will never have more than the barest minimum of a personality.

Another quality that appears at this age is conscience. Preschoolers view discipline in rule-defined, black-and-white terms; it is imposed from without and lacks any sort of shading. But if older children are asked, for example, whether one child should be punished for hitting another, they want to know more about the circumstances before passing judgment. As conscience develops, children begin to internalize the moral standards they have been taught, and in doing so, they adjust the rules to fit their own sense of justice. When preschoolers misbehave, they feel guilty because they fear getting caught, but older children feel guilty because they have violated their own rules of conduct.

Personal standards of achievement, some of which appear to last throughout life, are established as well. One study revealed, for example, that the degree of dependence observed in boys age six to 14 is not related to dependence in adulthood, but that striving for success at this age does predict a continuing effort toward achievement as adults. The same was found to be true of girls.

Whether they are prepared or not, at around the age of 12 or 13 children enter adolescence, which may be the most exciting and the most turbulent time of life. During a period that lasts for as much as a decade, the young person must adjust to rapid physical changes while at the same time struggling to carve out an adult identity. The central question the adolescent needs to answer is: Who am I? Formulating a coherent response is difficult, in part because the new adult body has not fully developed.

One of a child's main tasks in establishing an identity is to end the dependent relationship with mother and father. Some cultures reward independence more than others, however. For example, American children are expected to become self-supporting before choosing a mate; by contrast, in several Asian cultures and among the Arapesh in the mountains of New Guinea, the mate is often chosen by the family while bride and groom are still children living at home.

As they seek to define themselves, teenagers in Western cultures look for models of behavior, especially among their peers. This is not to say that parents are ignored. Some psychological studies suggest that, although well-adjusted children turn to peers for guidance in matters such as style of dress and taste in music, they continue to rely on parents and relatives as models on weighty issues involving education and careers. But the inclination to seek approval from peers, which first appears in the elementary school years, becomes more intense during early adolescence. It fades again as children approach adulthood.

The rapid physical changes of ado-

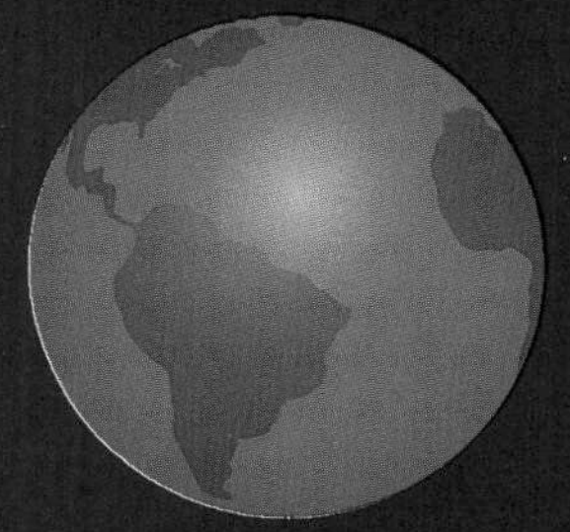

The Worldwide Face of Personality

The study of personality development has traditionally hinged on the assumption that within every human being dwells a universal psychic kernel. In addressing how and why personalities differ across cultures, many researchers therefore take as a given that people everywhere share the same basic mental framework and that the details—including the specifics of personality—are merely incidental, varying from culture to culture like regional dialects of a global language.

Scholars in the emerging field of cultural psychology, however, take a different view, one in which cultural variations are anything but incidental to psychology. Culture and psyche are, as Richard Shweder of the University of Chicago puts it, "seamlessly interconnected." According to this logic, psychology is not simply flavored but substantially organized and defined by its cultural context. Cultural psychologists hold that recognizing these basic psychological differences is essential to bridging gaps between peoples in a world fraught with ethnic conflict.

Instead of trying to apply Western models across societal boundaries, cultural psychologists focus on how a unique psychology arises from the singular combination of influences within each culture. As detailed on the following pages, these researchers examine such factors as the notion of self, the influence of language and the way it is acquired, and a culture's moral beliefs, all in the hope of understanding how the individual psyche forms and functions in different cultural settings.

lescence can have strong effects on the sense of self. Because adolescents are intensely aware of their appearance, they tend to be critical of the smallest flaws. Girls may develop exaggerated concerns about being overweight, leading to dangerous patterns of dieting, such as anorexia nervosa or bulimia (binge eating). Boys who mature early enjoy a physical and social advantage over slow-maturing peers, who may carry the feelings of inferiority for some time. Among girls, early maturing tends to be associated with a more positive self-image and a better overall adjustment, according to some studies, although the effects of differing rates of maturation are less pronounced than for boys.

Some children may retreat from the emotional stress of adolescence, taking refuge in exaggerated intellectualism, introspection, and asceticism. A few may be caught in a vicious cycle of rejection: Because they appear to lack confidence, they are rejected by their peers. This may lower self-esteem and lead to even greater social isolation. Studies have shown that the adolescents who are least worried about their peers' judgment are the most respected.

Adolescence, while full of pressures and worries, can be a restorative time as well. Psychologists have observed, for example, that during this period, the emotional scars of childhood may heal. A sympathetic girlfriend may help a boy with emotionally manipulative parents overcome a stressful family situation, and a girl from a demanding and competitive family may gain self-esteem from a boyfriend who admires her for her innate qualities and is not judgmental about her accomplishments.

In adolescence, a teenager may "try on" any number of different identities for brief periods, but in early adulthood this experimentation and confusion abates. One survey of college students reflected the process of stabilization: When asked questions designed to elicit commitment to an identity, only 11 percent of first-year

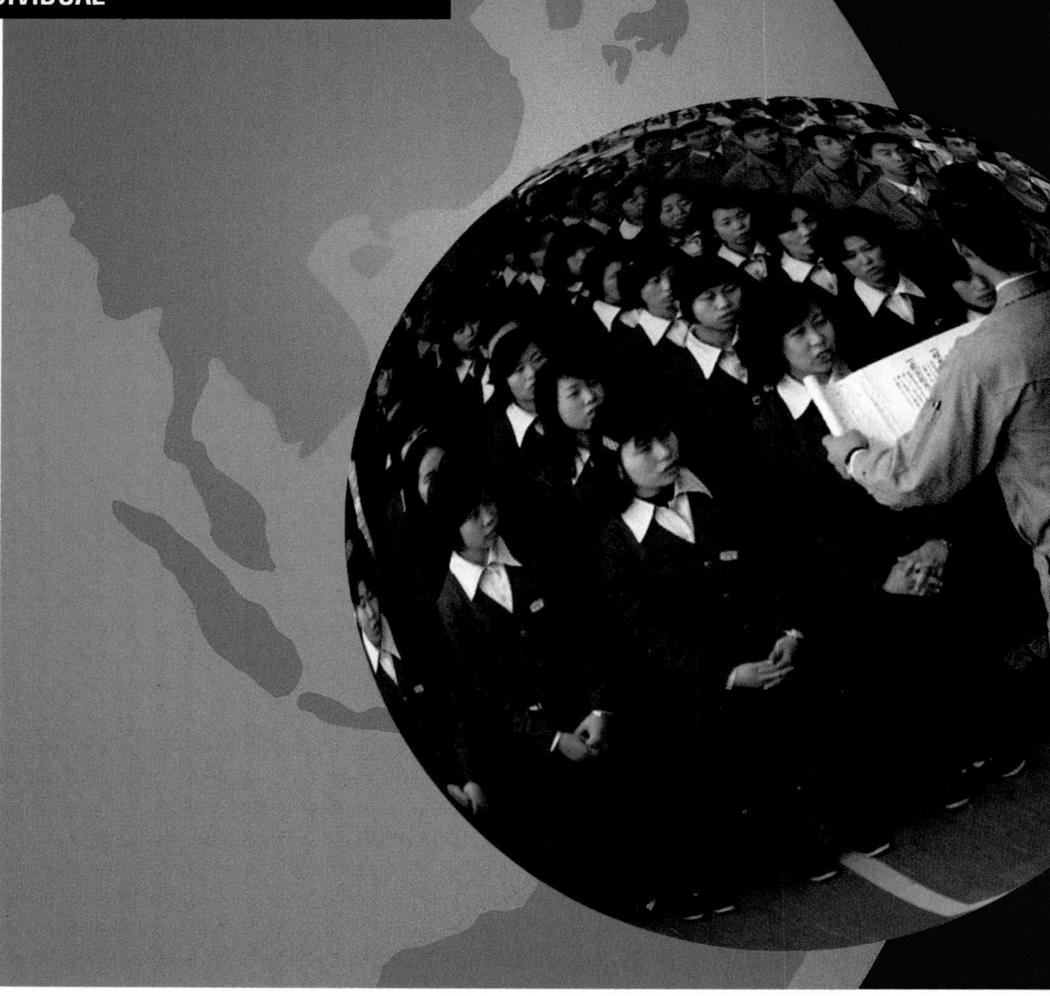

students responded positively, but by the end of senior year, 45 percent did so. In the United States, children are encouraged to become not just self-sufficient but self-supporting in their twenties—finding a job and settling down to the work of life.

Early adulthood is the time when the individual learns about living with another person and sharing experiences. Relations with the other sex change from what one writer has called "genital combat" to a union built on trust. Although many people say they intend never to marry, studies of the United States population indicate that about 96 percent do marry at some time.

There is no consistent evidence on types of personality that match well in marriage and no simple explanation for the timing of marriage. Typically, at some point between the ages of 20 and 30, people see themselves as ready to marry—perhaps because of peer pressure, family urging, or some particular event such as graduation from college or even the death of a parent. A large element of chance may be part of the process of choosing a spouse. People seem to marry whomever they are dating seriously when the moment of readiness occurs.

Marrying is usually the biggest decision of early adulthood, but having children brings on the biggest responsibility. According to U.S. data, nine out of 10 women have at least one child during their life, and the arrival of the firstborn, according to 83 percent of parents who responded to one survey, brings a "severe crisis" to the marital relationship.

The mother is usually the more strongly affected of the parents. If she has been working, she may have to curtail professional activities or leave her job temporarily. Typically, she assumes most of the burden of caring for the new child, which increases stress at a difficult time. Without a job, she also is likely to lose some independence and social contact with adults, making her economically and psychologically more dependent on her husband. In addition, husband and wife may discover for the first time that they have different ideas about how to raise children.

Despite all these stresses, most couples survive the trial. In fact, according to some recent studies, marriage tends to safeguard mental health, and married people are less likely than singles to be depressed or mentally disturbed.

As young adults grow older, physical changes occur that are a kind of obverse of adolescence. But the latter years bring profound psychological changes as well. Some people feel themselves adrift as they head toward and then enter retirement, but in most cases, this is a time of quiet satisfactions. With children grown and other

Differing Perspectives on the Sense of Self

In reassessing the links between society and personality, cultural psychology takes almost nothing for granted, least of all the concept of personality. Recognizing that even the idea of what makes a person can vary from society to society, cultural psychologists have tried to divest themselves of their own notions of personality before interpreting those held by others.

Cultural psychologists Hazel Markus and Shinobu Kitayama have pointed out, for example, that in most Asian societies, the self is usually connected to the group (*left*). Even the Japanese word for self, *jibun*, refers to "one's share of the shared life space." But most Western cultures consider the self as an independent and autonomous force, separate from its context.

Markus and Kitayama acknowledge that supposedly individualistic Americans often act interdependently, just as members of generally group-oriented Asian societies are capable of genuinely autonomous action. But they have urged colleagues in related fields to recognize the considerable consequences that these divergent models of self could have for an individual's thoughts, emotions, and motives—parts of what we think of as personality.

Some of those consequences were evident in a study in which subjects from two cultures were asked to give descriptions of people they knew. Americans described their acquaintances with statements such as "She is friendly," indicating a view of people as possessing inherent character traits that appear in a wide variety of circumstances. Natives of India, on the other hand, usually spoke of their friends in terms of specific contexts and actions—"She brings cakes to my family on festival days," for example, suggesting a definition of people by their surroundings and their relationship to others, rather than by their intrinsic qualities.

These differing perspectives can be a source of bewilderment when cultures mix. An American host offering an Asian guest a choice of beverages, for instance, could easily interpret the visitor's noncommittal response as self-effacing behavior or a lack of decisiveness. In fact, the guest's reaction may spring from the expectation prevalent among Asians that the role of the gracious host is to choose well for the guest.

pressures lessened or removed, it may also be a time to pursue some long-delayed ambitions or to show aspects of personality—competitiveness in a woman, perhaps, or domesticity in a man—that had been largely discouraged by stereotyped sex roles.

Tracing the course of behavioral development with anything like a surveyor's precision is a major research challenge, and most investigators would concede that much work remains to be done. Getting at the deeper dynamics of personality, the how and why beneath the what, is a more formidable job still. The most obvious complication is the sheer multiplicity and variety of environmental influences—parents, siblings, peers, teachers, socioeconomic stratum, events such as illness or divorce, and many other particulars in a developing individual's life. Nonspecific factors such as the overall poverty or richness of the environment also may be important.

During the early 1960s, for example, a group of researchers studied the effect on orphans of the nonstimulating surroundings typical of the institutions where they grew up. The children—who were kept in cribs in a partitioned space that minimized interaction with adults as well as communication between infants—exhibited few signs of abnormality before four months. By eight months, however, most of the orphans were less interested in toys than is typical of other children. As they approached their first birthday, many of the orphans acquired the body-rocking movements characteristic of disturbed children. They also were slower than normal to develop language. An observer described one of these children as marked by "soberness," a "forlorn appearance," and "lack of animation." Whether these particular individuals were able to overcome their bleak beginnings is not clear, but many others have surmounted early hardships to lead a normal life.

To some extent, the degree of stim-

ulation of young children and their contact with adults may be culturally determined. For example, Guatemalan children, who spend their early years close to their mother but typically in a dark hut with no toys to distract them, appear quiet and dull, even listless, by North American standards. In Japan, mothers soothe their babies into silence and as a result, the infants are much less likely than American babies to make babbling sounds and to vocalize.

The influence of culture, though subtle in infancy, becomes an increasingly powerful force up to age five or so, so that even the very young typically adopt some of the basic personality traits that their society values over others. Middle-class American children, for example, learn independence at an early age. By contrast, children raised in the Zuni or Hopi Native American culture of the Southwest tend to be less competitive and more cooperative: Pueblo Indians emphasize social harmony and frown on individuals who place their own interests ahead of those of the group.

Researchers have found that children usually become aware of their ethnic or racial status by the age of four or five. As discovered in 1939 in the United States, children in ethnic minority groups may acquire a negative image of themselves, reflecting a bias of the culture in which they live. A similar investigation 30 years later, however, revealed that the tendency toward an unfavorable self-image had begun to diminish, largely because of the ethnic pride instilled by the civil rights movement of the 1960s. But feelings of negative self-worth that do survive can contribute to below-normal achievement in school. (Interestingly, studies have shown that children who exhibit racial intolerance—an outlook that, like an individual's self-awareness of status, is usually learned at an early age—tend to be more rigid and poorer at solving problems than their peers.)

Among the many environmental factors that shape behavior, the child-raising practices of the parents have traditionally been seen as paramount. Researchers have conducted many studies to find links between parenting styles and the personality of the child. Such investigations are difficult, because what goes on in a family cannot always be fathomed by simply interviewing the parents, asking them to fill out questionnaires, or even using structured observation sessions.

Some researchers think they have found clear cause-and-effect patterns, however. One study hypothesizes three categories. So-called authoritarian parenting—in which the adults impose many rules on the children, demand strict obedience, yet do not bother to explain the reasons for all the regulations—is said to produce

Decoding the World of Talk

Cultural psychologists and other researchers are increasingly focusing on the role of language in cultural assimilation. As children learn to use language the way that adults do, says linguistics professor Patricia Clancy of the University of California at Santa Barbara, they "internalize the cultural values that are making adults use language that way in the first place."

In middle-class Anglo-American families, for example, children are generally treated as partners in conversation even before they can speak. Adults commonly speak to them in simplified "baby talk" and translate what children say—even an infant's meaningless gurgles—into proper speech for them. These practices, according to linguistic anthropologists Bambi Schieffelin and Elinor Ochs, impart a cultural lesson as well as a linguistic one, teaching children that adults will make allowances for their limited abilities and will adjust situations accordingly. This idea is then integrated into these children's world view and their behavior, becoming part of a characteristically "American" personality.

This particular lesson, say Schieffelin and Ochs, is far from universal. The Kaluli people of Papua New Guinea (*left, with Schieffelin*), for instance, believe that babies "have no understanding." Adults, therefore, rarely speak directly to babies or attribute any meaning to their utterances. Mothers teach young ones to talk by speaking for them—not by interpreting their supposed wishes but by expressing what the mother feels should be said, a practice that teaches children that they will be expected to fit adult situations rather than vice versa.

Other studies have shown that American mothers are inclined to verbally label the parts of toys their children play with; at 19 months, American babies have nearly twice the vocabulary of their Japanese counterparts. Japanese mothers tend to use toys to rehearse social rituals with their children, often without ever teaching them the name of the object. Despite the differences, each set of methods enables children to function properly within their own cultural boundaries: American children are indoctrinated with their culture's emphasis on performance skills, while Japanese children are taught the importance of social interaction.

children who are moody, unfriendly, and easily annoyed. Permissive parenting—in which the adults exert little control over children, make few demands, and encourage the expression of feelings and impulses—is said to produce children who are low in self-reliance, self-control, and achievement. Authoritative parenting—yielding a flexible environment in which the children are given a good deal of freedom but rules are enforced (and explained)—is said to produce cheerful, self-reliant, self-controlled, and socially responsive children, oriented toward achievement.

This three-category scheme is not universally accepted. Indeed, many researchers believe that all such efforts are fundamentally flawed. Parenting style, they say, is not a reliable indicator of how personality will develop, and certainly the history of the behavioral sciences suggests that finding simple personality predictors will not be easy.

One cautionary lesson is a theory based on the birth rank of siblings. It was first proposed by the psychoanalyst Alfred Adler, a contemporary of Sigmund Freud. According to Adler, personal qualities such as competitiveness, humor, and diligence are determined primarily by where a child ranks among brothers and sisters. The firstborn will be ambitious, responsible, and early to mature—probably because parents devote so much concentrated attention to the oldest child. The second and other mid-ranked children will often be overshadowed by the older siblings, and thus resentful, but quick to compromise and find pragmatic solutions. Finally, the baby of the family is likely to be irresponsible and clownish. The simplicity and apparent common sense of this guide to personality has given it wide appeal. But research has shown that it fails to predict consistently what kind of adults these children will grow up to be.

Another popular assumption about family dynamics is that the adults determine the parent-child relation-

ship—that the child, in effect, is a passive participant. That view, too, is simplistic: Much research has shown that a child's personality must be taken into account as well.

One of the most ambitious probes of the issue was launched in the 1960s by a group of New York physicians—Alexander Thomas of the New York University Medical Center, Stella Chess of Bellevue Hospital in New York City, and Herbert Birch, a professor of pediatrics at the Albert Einstein College of Medicine in New York. These three felt that psychological theories of the day put too much responsibility on the mother and father, seeming to blame them for every emotional disturbance. As evidence to the contrary, they noted that some children who were raised in circumstances of severe family disorganization and who received poor parental care appeared to be largely unaffected, showing no personality disturbances. The opposite was also true: Children with seemingly normal upbringings sometimes displayed serious psychological problems.

To learn more about how personality emerges and develops, the New York physicians set down nine categories of behavior to measure. Their checklist included motor activity, degree of regularity in sleeping and eating, response to a new object or person, sensitivity to stimuli, positive or negative mood, and other measures of temperament. The doctors recruited the parents of 141 children and asked them to provide detailed information about their sons and daughters; later they followed up with interviews of teachers and other observers. They tracked 136 children for more than a decade, keeping tabs on them through adolescence. (Because of this long-term approach, the project became known as the New York Longitudinal Study.)

When they classified the children according to patterns of behavior, the researchers found that they could place most of them—65 percent—into three clusters, clearly distinct even in infancy. (The rest of the children exhibited traits that were too varied to be grouped.) The largest of the three well-defined clusters—40 percent of all the children—was labeled "easy." As babies, these "easy" children quickly settled down to a regular pattern of sleeping and eating, exhibited a positive mood, and adapted readily to changes in their routine. Very different qualities marked another category—about 10 percent of the children—which the doctors labeled "difficult." They did not eat or sleep on a regular schedule, tended to withdraw from anything new in the environment, disliked change, cried a good deal, and would often throw a tantrum when frustrated. The third of the clusters was labeled "slow to

The Parameters of Right and Wrong

Personality is generally understood to be an enduring pattern of attitudes, values, and behavior. Cultural psychologists are thus interested in tracing how people incorporate the value systems and moral codes defined by their cultures into their individual patterns. According to most theorists, men and women everywhere base moral decisions upon whether someone is harmed, whether rights are violated, and whether justice is served. But while such a moral code may be a feature of most societies—making it unacceptable around the world, for example, to hurt an innocent victim (*left*)—cultural psychologists believe that other notions of morality centered on cultural standards may generate significant differences in individual judgments of what is right or wrong.

Richard Shweder, for one, has proposed an alternative model of morality that goes beyond the harm, rights, and justice code familiar in the Western tradition—which he calls the ethic of autonomy. His model also includes an ethic of community, in which people consider violations of honor and respect to be moral offenses, and an ethic of divinity, which deems issues of personal sanctity and purity—such as the eating restrictions outlined in the Old Testament—to be part of the moral landscape.

Jonathan Haidt of the University of Chicago designed a test of Shweder's model in which he evaluated how six groups of adults and children in the United States and Brazil reacted to stories that told of harmless but potentially offensive actions. Haidt reasoned that if the moral domain is limited to those actions that are perceived as harmful or unjust, these stories—including one of a woman using an old flag to clean a bathroom—would not evoke a moral response. He discovered, however, that many subjects in the study, while often acknowledging that the actions described were neither harmful nor unjust, nevertheless felt them to be morally reprehensible. Haidt found that the stories were most moralized by the least cosmopolitan subjects—those from a poor city in northeastern Brazil—and least moralized by a group of college students from an elite American university. His results lend credence to cultural psychologists' theory that moral judgment, like other psychological processes, can operate differently in different populations.

warm up." Babies in this group were less active than the others, slow to respond to new stimuli, and somewhat negative in mood.

The New York physicians concluded that the "easy" children responded to a variety of child-rearing styles, but "difficult" children challenged parents from the outset. It takes sustained, consistent instruction, they said, to help such children adjust to society. The "slow to warm up" children also required patience and had to be allowed to develop at their own pace. The overall point made by the New York group was the need to recognize the importance of "the interaction between the child's own characteristics and his environment. If the two influences are harmonized, one can expect healthy development of the child; if they are dissonant, behavioral problems are almost sure to ensue."

In recent decades, a number of investigators have explored the two-way nature of the parent-child relationship. A familiar illustration of children's power is the tyranny a newborn can wield over young parents by crying. As one psychologist expresses it: "There is almost no effort we will not expend, no device we will not employ, to change a crying baby into a smiling one—or just a quiet one." If crying persists beyond a parent's endurance, it may have tragic consequences. Research studies from the early 1970s found that in cases of child battering, the parents often said that the abused child was constantly fussing or had a strange, irritating cry. While such claims do not excuse the parents' behavior, they may in fact be truthful. And psychologists have noticed that abusive parents tend to focus their wrath on just one child within the family—suggesting, again, that there may be something about the individual child's behavior that contributes to the pattern of violence.

The experience of abusive families does not represent the norm, of course, but all children have ways of influencing their own environment. Studies of newborns have found that

whether a baby smiles or frets when first brought to the mother is an important determinant of how interactions between the two of them will unfold. Later on, as children become attached to their parents, they learn ways to keep the parents on a short leash, if that is what they desire. Some studies have shown that children start about 50 percent of interactions with their parents. They also may resist parental guidance—perhaps by flashing a winning smile while ignoring what they do not want to hear. Over the long haul, such opposition can change the parents' goals and expectations for their offspring, causing the adults to give up on what has become a frustrating effort to direct their children in a particular way.

Stanford University psychologist Albert Bandura has devoted his career to exploring the manner in which humans shape environmental forces even as they are controlled by those forces. He calls the process "reciprocal determinism," and as a small example of how it works, he points to television-viewing behavior. People have one clear control over their televised environment: They choose what to watch from among the programs on the television schedule. Within this limited repertoire, they also help indirectly to determine the future television schedule, since their viewing preferences may be registered by television ratings, which are carefully considered by programmers in putting together a slate of offerings. Thus, viewing behavior, viewer preferences, and televised programming all affect each other reciprocally.

In Bandura's view, most human behavior is developed through learning that involves self-generated influences. Bandura's theory is founded on what he calls the "self system," which regulates behavior by a continuous process of self-observation, making judgments, and responding to self-behavior. For example, a person may observe her performance at work in terms of such factors as productivity or originality; she may judge the performance according to her standards or by how it compares to the performance of other people; and she may reward or punish herself on the basis of the judgment.

Bandura and his colleagues have carried out many experiments demonstrating how human behavior can be modified by changing personal expectations. Providing plentiful self-incentives is the key. In one experiment, for example, he showed that children who were having trouble with mathematics were more likely to gain proficiency if they set a series of near-term goals that allowed immediate self-evaluation rather than setting larger goals that took longer to reach.

Human behavior, according to Bandura, has a kind of swirling fluidity

The Dynamics of Ethnicity

Cultural psychologists have looked with increasing interest at the psychological consequences of immigration and acculturation. At the heart of their studies are questions of identity: If psyche and culture are "seamlessly interconnected," what happens to the psyche when it is put into a new cultural setting?

Recent work has examined how the personalities of immigrants and their descendants change in new surroundings. A 1990 study compared the family patterns of Chinese immigrants in the United States and Australia with Anglo families in each of these cultures and with a control group of Chinese families in Hong Kong. As might be expected, the spirit within the Hong Kong households was essentially communal, whereas that among the Anglo families tended to promote individualism and autonomy. As for the immigrant families in both Australia and the United States, they turned out to be remarkably alike in showing signs of accommodation to the more individualistic attitudes of the host country—becoming involved more often, for example, in activities outside the family. Yet even immigrant families of long standing retained important elements of their traditional Chinese family structure, such as more of an insistence on conformity of opinion.

Cultural psychologists Marcelo and Carola Suarez-Orozco have obtained similar results in a comparative study of age-matched groups of native Mexicans, recent Mexican immigrants to the United States, and second-generation Mexican Americans. For adolescents in all three groups, they found that family remained the dominant frame of reference, as compared with a control sample of non-Latino American youths, for whom peers were equally influential. However, youths of Mexican extraction living in the United States were virtually indistinguishable from other Americans of their age when measured on achievement motivation. This finding suggests that immigrants may embrace a new culture's yardsticks for success in society at large more willingly than they adopt foreign standards for matters closer to home.

that is almost dizzying. He stresses behavior's malleability—all the ways it can be changed by learning. But a number of studies have shown that basic behavioral traits exhibit considerable inertia. For example, the New York Longitudinal Study, while it focused on the parent-child relationship, also produced a large amount of data indicating that some behavioral traits seen early in life "tended to persist" through childhood. A child called Donald, for example, was highly active from birth. At the age of three months he wriggled in his crib; at 12 months he squirmed while being dressed; and at 15 months his parents reported that they had to chase after him constantly to keep him out of trouble. When he went to school at the age of seven, Donald had difficulty paying attention to the teachers and tended to disrupt the class.

In 1968 two psychologists at the University of California at Berkeley, Jack and Jeanne Block, launched a more direct and even more protracted study of the persistence of behavioral traits—a true investigatory epic. For their project, the Blocks selected a group of more than 100 three-year-olds, and they followed them with regular evaluations through the age of 23. The psychologists did not find a one-for-one correlation between preschool and adult behavior, but they did observe a "coherence" in responses over time, suggesting that personality develops in a continuous fashion. For example, children who scored high on self-esteem in childhood (as measured by the degree to which descriptions of themselves matched descriptions of an "ideal self") generally scored high in adulthood as well.

However, the Blocks noticed some big differences between the sexes. Girls maintained a steady self-image throughout adolescence, while boys went through a period of image "restructuring" between ages 14 and 18. In adulthood, the sexes diverged further, with women gradually dropping in self-esteem, while men remained stable. Interestingly, there was no correlation between high IQ test scores and high rank in self-esteem.

On the negative side, the Blocks also discovered childhood traits that pointed toward later drug use and depression. For example, girls who would later become depressive tended to be shy and reserved at age seven, while boys who would suffer from depression at a later stage were aggressive at seven.

The Blocks' documentation of the continuity of some traits seemed to shed light on one of the most fundamental issues in the behavioral sciences. Its essence was summed up in two opposed words popularized by the 19th-century British scientist Francis Galton: nature versus nurture.

Galton, a genius in a family of geniuses, suspected that many behavioral traits and abilities were inherited—that they were due primarily to the natural or biological endowment of the individual rather than to the individual's upbringing, social circumstances, or other elements of nurture. To get at the heart of the matter, he pored over written histories of families and conducted studies of twins and siblings who had been separated by adoption and raised apart. His labors convinced him that many traits could indeed be described as predispositions, or inheritances. "Nature," he said, "prevails enormously over nurture." Charles Darwin, the great evolutionist and Galton's cousin, endorsed this view: "I am inclined to agree with Francis Galton in believing that education and environment produce only a small effect on the mind of anyone, and that most of our qualities are innate."

The pendulum swung the other way in the 20th century, partly because of the influence of the behaviorist school of psychology, which argued that practically all behavior was acquired through learning, and also because of revulsion at the pseudogenetic theories of the Nazis, who killed millions of Jews, Gypsies, and Slavs because of what the Nazis deemed inferior inheritance. But genetics could not be ignored. Too much evidence indicated that environmental factors alone were insufficient to account for behavioral differences among people. Today, the role of the genes is very much on the minds of psychologists.

One way to explore the influence of genes is to look at siblings—pairs of brothers and sisters. Like parent and child, they share about half of their genes. In the 1980s, two psychologists at Pennsylvania State University, Judy Dunn and Robert Plomin, pulled together a broad range of statistical information bearing on sibling similarities and differences. On some physical measures, such as weight and height, siblings match up with a correlation of about 50 percent.

The correlation figure does not refer to individuals. Instead, it is a mathematical way of expressing variances in populations—in this case, sibling differences in relation to the variance that would be seen among randomly chosen pairs in the general population. A correlation of 0 would indicate that, as a group, siblings are no more alike than random pairs, whereas a correlation of 1 would mean that, as a group, siblings are exactly alike.

A .5 correlation for weight and height suggests that the variances in these characteristics are almost entirely determined by the genes, as siblings have about 50 percent of their genetic endowment in common. But on other measures such as vocabulary or intelligence tests, siblings exhibit a much lower correlation. One set of studies found, for example, that siblings scored a .35 correlation on vocabulary, .25 on verbal fluency, and .15 on memory ability.

In measures of personality, the research again revealed low correlations. The largest study examined personality in terms of two major clusters of factors: extraversion (which encompasses such factors as sociability, liveliness, and impulsiveness) and neuroticism (which includes such signs of instability as anxiousness, moodiness, and irritability). The sibling correlations were .25 for extraversion and a mere .07 for neuroticism. Studies have found higher correlations, however—up to .4—for factors that are more like attitudes than measures of personality; among such attitudinal traits are traditionalism (meaning conformity or conservativeness) and tolerance for ambiguity. But the average sibling correlation for personality, according to Dunn and Plomin, is a mere .15—far below the .5 sibling correlation that would be the case if personality were entirely controlled by the genes.

Fortunately for the behavioral sciences, nature and society have combined to provide a powerful research tool for isolating the influences of genes and environment: identical twins or triplets who are raised apart. Such subjects share 100 percent of their genes; they are developed from a single fertilized egg that split shortly after conception. When such twins or triplets are separated after birth and raised in different adoptive families, the contribution of genes to their physical and behavioral makeup becomes clear. Since they are genetically identical, differences must be attributed to their different environments.

Since 1979, a group of psychologists led by Thomas Bouchard Jr. at the University of Minnesota have been collecting data on identical twins and triplets who were raised apart. More than 100 of these unusual sets have been examined so far, and the researchers have compiled a huge mass of information—about physical characteristics, mental abilities, lifestyles, tastes, personality, and much more. (For comparative purposes, the Minnesota project also includes identical twins raised together and fraternal twins raised both apart and together.)

From the start, the Minnesota investigators have found remarkable

NASA's Mercury astronauts—all seven of them firstborn sons—epitomize the qualities that some researchers think stem from being the oldest child in a family. Firstborns tend to be hard-driving, achievement oriented, and responsible. Eager to assume adult leadership roles, they often mature faster psychologically than subsequent offspring. One explanation may be that firstborns typically receive the lion's share of parents' attention, as well as bearing the brunt of their expectations.

similarities in identical siblings who were entirely unaware of each other's existence until brought together by the study. For example, only two individuals among all those examined by Bouchard's team have shown a fear of entering the closed acoustical chamber where interviews are conducted; those two were identical twins raised apart. Similar matches have turned up for twins who giggle, tell amusing anecdotes, devote themselves to dogs, fear water, collect guns, and captain volunteer fire departments. That such specific characteristics, predilections, and life choices repeatedly appear in twins raised apart seems more than coincidental.

The same parallelism applies to psychological difficulties, as exemplified by the case of Beth and Amy. These identical twins went to different adoptive families soon after their birth, and each seemed normal at first. But problems began to appear after their first birthday, and by the age of 10 both had been diagnosed as suffering from "character disturbances," "limited self-definition," and retarded development.

The University of Minnesota researchers focused on a general measure called heritability, which—like the correlation statistic—applies to large groups rather than to individuals. Heritability is defined as the estimate of the amount of variation in a population that is due to genetic variation. In such physical matters as body weight, brain wave patterns, and susceptibility to certain illnesses, the analysis of identical siblings reared apart indicates very high heritability; that is, almost all observed variation can be attributed to genetic factors. For IQ, the estimated heritability is somewhat lower—about 70 percent. For personality traits—which in the Minnesota study are measured by standard tests that determine the degree of introversion or extraversion, flexibility, acceptance of traditional values, aggressiveness, and many other characteristics—heritability is estimated at about 50 percent. In other words, genes explain about half of the observed variation in personality. Environment explains the rest.

Other studies of twins have yielded the same 50-50 estimate for genetic and environmental contributions to personality. In addition to arriving at a solid estimate for this long-debated matter, the various studies carried out by researchers in the field of behavioral genetics have yielded an important insight into the environmental component of personality formation:

A given family environment does not operate uniformly, it seems. This discovery reverses a long-held belief. "For decades," write Penn State's Dunn and Plomin, "we were misled by the resemblance within families. Because heredity was not given its due, it was assumed that sibling similarity is caused by environmental factors shared by children growing up in the same family. Siblings resemble each other for genetic reasons, however, not for environmental reasons. That is, siblings are similar, but they are just as similar if they are adopted apart and reared in different families. Growing up in the same family is not responsible for their resemblance. What runs in families is DNA, not shared experiences in the family."

This finding has the effect of bringing the individual to the fore of the behavioral sciences. As Dunn and Plomin put it, "Environmental influences that affect development operate on an individual-by-individual basis, not on a family-by-family basis." Everyone has his or her own self-made, customized environment within a family—what behavioral scientists call a microenvironment. Psychologist Sandra Scarr of the University of Virginia in Charlottesville, a leading researcher in the field, observes: "Microenvironments are largely the construction of individual family members in the way they evoke responses from others, actively select or ignore opportunities, and construct their own experiences."

The modern view of personality formation is thus wonderfully dynamic—a never-ending, individual-centered interplay of genes and the world. Parents remain a key part of the picture, but their contribution is seen in more generalized terms than used to be the case. In the disarming phrase of Sandra Scarr, parents need to be "good enough," meaning that they do not need to be perfect, tirelessly engaged in promoting their child's well-being (and often afflicted with guilt because they see themselves as falling short). The fact is, perfection would not make a difference. "Good enough, ordinary parents probably have the same effects on their children's development as culturally defined super-parents." A good-enough environment, she adds, is one that "supports children's development to become themselves." It's as simple—and subtle—as that.

3

Extremes of Personality

Gayle was not Gayle. That much was clear to neurologist Bruce Dobkin almost as soon as she and her husband Roger arrived at his office. Dobkin had examined Gayle months earlier, after she suffered a brain injury when Roger's car slammed into a pickup truck that ran a red light. Gayle, riding in the passenger seat, had been flung against the windshield, shattering it with her forehead. The blow knocked her unconscious, but a brain scan indicated nothing more severe than mild swelling in the frontal lobes. She was discharged from the hospital within a week and went home to celebrate her 35th birthday and resume her life as a homemaker, amateur sculptor, and mother of two small children. Dr. Dobkin had found her somewhat confused and forgetful in the wake of the accident, but such symptoms were common enough in cases of head trauma. Though her manner at the time had been subdued, even withdrawn, that seemed to jibe with her husband's description of her as a "modest, introspective" person.

Now, however, Gayle was something else altogether. "It's so good to see you," she gushed, throwing her arms around the doctor and pressing against him while Roger looked on in dismay. As Dobkin pulled free, Gayle began to chatter, pouring out disconnected ideas in a nonstop stream—all the while touching and stroking her embarrassed husband's leg. Finally, Dobkin directed her to the examination table and peered into her eyes with an ophthalmoscope, checking for signs of brain swelling. She brushed her cheek against his, then unbuttoned her blouse and said, "Will you listen to my heart?"

Gayle's hyperactive, eroticized behavior had begun only a week or two earlier. During the first 10 weeks after the accident, she had grown progressively more withdrawn, slipping into depression and sleeping away the afternoons. Then, without warning, the apathy abruptly gave way to boundless energy—especially in the matter of sex. In their bedroom at night, she had been demanding endless lovemaking from Roger, the more adventurous the better. She would then arise and go to her studio where, instead of working on sculptures of faces as had been her custom, she created male torsos complete with exaggerated sexual organs. Daytime brought no diminution in her sex drive, and her strange behavior even spilled beyond the family. On several occasions when she and Roger were with other people, she had made explicit sexual remarks. At a party the week before, both female and male friends were targets of her advances and had difficulty fending her off.

Roger was now desperate, wondering if he would ever regain the quiet, demure wife he had known through 12 years of marriage. After consulting with a psychiatrist, Dr. Dobkin offered hope. He and his colleague suspected that Gayle's behavior stemmed from damage to a pathway between an area of the brain responsible for the reproductive drive and another area that exerts control over sexual responsiveness. Animal studies have shown that electrical stimulation of certain clumps of nerve cells in the frontal lobes induces an almost frantic urge to copulate. Other experiments indicate that control of the sex drive depends on the neurotransmitter dopamine. Too little dopamine inhibits the sex drive, but too much can force a person's erotic urges into overdrive.

In Gayle's case, the doctors suspected that the frontal-lobe injuries were causing her dopamine levels to fluctuate erratically. After some experimentation, they prescribed the drug carbamazepine, ordinarily used in cases of epilepsy but sometimes effective in calming agitated behavior resulting from head trauma. It worked like magic. Within two weeks, the uncontrolled sexual cravings disappeared, and the modest Gayle returned.

Gayle's case is a dramatic instance of personality gone awry. What happened to her is rare, indeed extraordinary. But extremes of personality —attitudes and habits sufficiently aberrant to warrant the psychiatric label *disorder*—are not uncommon. Genes and environmental influences conspire over periods of years or even decades to do to millions of individuals what an automobile accident did to Gayle in a matter of weeks: produce a pattern of behavior that interferes with the normal routine of daily activities or is otherwise harmful to the afflicted person, and sometimes harmful to other people as well.

Personality disorders generally emerge during adolescence or during a person's early twenties, and some abate later in life. The disorders come in many forms, and various types are often combined in an individual, compounding the diagnostic difficulties. Sufferers may be relentlessly aggressive or paralyzed by shyness. They may be incorrigibly self-dramatizing or utterly dependent on others. They may be devoid of visible emotion or so buffeted by mood swings that they find it practically impossible to sustain a relationship. Some people afflicted with a personality disorder are ruled by beliefs in magical powers, some by an overwhelming fear of rejection, and some by a perpetual suspicion of everyone around them. Cer-

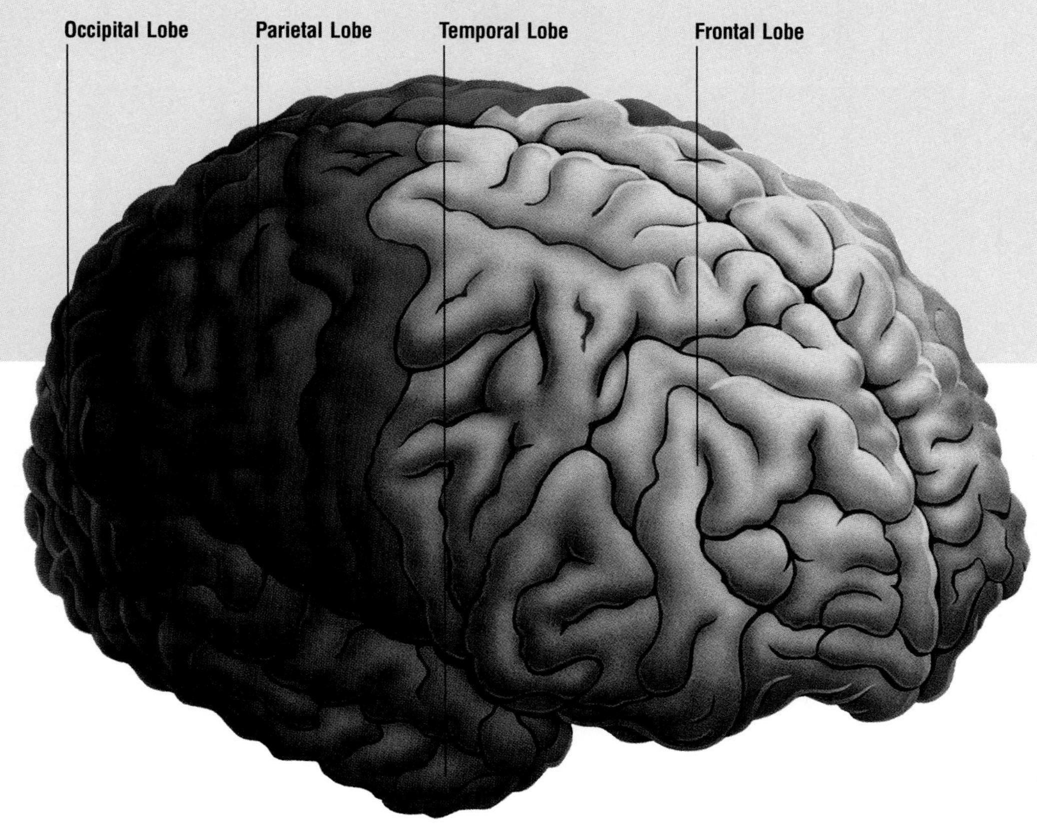

The brain's most recognizable feature is its wrinkled outer layer, the cerebral cortex *(left)*, the processing center for the most highly evolved human functions. Only an eighth of an inch thick, the cortex consists of two hemispheres, each divided into four lobes. In general, the left hemisphere is associated with language, logical analysis, and detailed perceptual and conceptual tasks; the right side, with spatial perception, imagination, and intuitive insight. Each lobe also oversees specific operations: The frontal lobes handle decision making; the parietal lobes govern sensory perception; the temporal lobes play a role in communication, hearing, and memory; and the occipital lobes are mostly devoted to vision.

tain personality disorders seem to affect women particularly often; others are concentrated among men. Some are more easily treated than others, but treatment is almost always desirable. Left to fester, personality disorders can make victims virtually unemployable, propel them toward crime and violence, or lead them into drug addiction. In their most extreme forms, the disorders can lead their victims to suicide.

Personality disorders occupy a middle position on the psychological spectrum. Their effects are typically less incapacitating than mental illnesses such as schizophrenia or manic-depressive disorder, which involve a disconnection from reality. On the other hand, personality disorders tend to be more pernicious than eccentricity, in the usual sense of the term. All societies have oddballs—people whose behavior is, as the word *eccentric* indicates, off-center. Great Britain has always boasted a rich supply of characters whose antics provoke wondering amusement. One famous case was Thomas Birch, an 18th-century librarian who costumed himself as a tree when fishing; another was a world-roving squire named Charles Waterton who, during trips to the tropics, would lie in his hammock with one foot bared to the night air in the hope that his big toe would be sucked by a vampire bat.

However cockeyed their view of the world, such people seem generally content. A recent study by a clinical psychologist at Royal Edinburgh Hospital concluded that only one eccentric in four shows signs of a personality disorder. Most, in fact, seem to be robust psychological specimens: The Edinburgh study found that eccentrics show above-average intelligence, creativity, health, and happiness.

Although personality disorders represent a troubled mental midground, some of their symptoms can be seen at times in almost everyone, if only fleetingly and in mild degree. For example, many people experience anxiety when faced with speaking in public: Their hands tremble, they grow dizzy or have trouble breathing, their heart pounds, and they may feel nau-

ECCENTRICS THEN AND NOW. The epitome of the modern eccentric, literary maverick Hunter Thompson, author of *Fear and Loathing in Las Vegas,* takes aim at his snowbound typewriter near his home in Woody Creek, Colorado *(above).* Calling himself the "champion of fun," Thompson has been known to videotape an assortment of his shenanigans, including setting a Christmas tree ablaze in his fireplace. A more respected figure, Britain's Charles Waterton, shown at left in an 1824 portrait, was a renowned traveler and naturalist but also one of his century's most famous eccentrics. He poses here with a preserved bird and a stuffed cat's head resting on a book.

seated. But the feelings of panic pass. By contrast, for someone with a personality disorder, anxiety can reach the point of governing almost every action and behavior. In the workplace, for instance, such a person who was offered a promotion that involved giving presentations before groups of people would use any excuse to avoid what ought to have been a positive career move—and, if pushed to it, would probably quit rather than accept this terrifying new responsibility.

Truly crippling terrors often fall into categories that psychologists classify as more serious than personality disorders. One example is the syndrome known as agoraphobia (literally, "fear of open places"). For an agoraphobe, leaving the house and going out into the world—if only to the store or to see a friend—may be impossible. A sufferer described it this way: "I have put my coat on hundreds of times and got as far as opening the door and standing on the doorstep. But I can't go any farther. You get this fear in your body and it puts you in a panic. If somebody speaks to you, you can't answer them because nothing will come, and so the panic gets worse. The farther you go away from the house, the worse it gets."

Although standard psychiatric manuals put severe problems such as agoraphobia in a separate grouping from personality disorders, there is some debate as to whether the two categories may be related—stemming, say, from a common biological or psychological origin. In any event, they do share the characteristic of an amplification of normal feelings: Suspicion is inflated almost to a sense of universal threat, or paranoia; desire for approval becomes an insatiable need; daydreaming is elevated into an elaborate fantasy world.

Some people with personality disorders are aware that they have a serious problem and are much distressed by it. Others are not even aware of a problem. As a rule, personality disorders result in far more anguish for the person's friends, family, and co-workers than for the person needing professional attention. When someone with a personality disorder sees a doctor, it is typically at the insistence of a spouse or an employer. The person will often be uncooperative, perhaps complaining loudly about a demanding spouse or a vindictive boss. Some patients will argue that their supposedly dysfunctional behavior—extreme competitiveness or perfectionism or mistrust of others, for example—has brought them recognition, money, and personal peace.

Even when examining doctors detect clear signs of aberrant behavior, they are often hesitant to diagnose a personality disorder, for fear of seeming arbitrary or of being perceived as moral police. To alleviate such concerns, psychiatry has developed elaborate diagnostic guidelines spelling out symptoms of personality disorders. The guidelines recognize 11 main disorders and group them into three clusters. Altogether, they embrace a very broad range of behaviors, a few of them close to the boundary of full-blown mental illness.

One cluster includes disorders that are particularly associated with fearfulness and anxiety.

Obsessive-compulsive personality disorder, diagnosed more frequently in males than in females, is characterized by a ceaseless, inflexible striving for perfection. To have this affliction, Austrian psychoanalyst Wilhelm Reich once commented, is to be a "living machine." People with the disorder—which first manifests itself in early adulthood—typically center their lives around work, pursuing it to the point of self-enslavement. Yet they are inefficient and indecisive, so preoccupied with rules, lists, and schedules that the point of what they are supposed to be doing is lost. Often, obsessive-compulsives shine brightly as middle-level managers, but their hesitations, their rigidity, and their inability to take a broad view of issues usually limits their career prospects.

In their conversational style, people with the disorder tend to be stiff, humorless, and formal, very precise in their choice of words, lacking in spontaneity. They place great weight on logic and the intellect, and they disapprove of emotionality in others. They are also very sensitive to criticism, especially from someone with higher status or authority.

Most psychiatrists make a point of distinguishing this personality disorder from a more severe condition with almost the same name: obsessive-compulsive disorder, whose sufferers find themselves trapped in repetitive habits or thoughts for which they can offer no explanation. (The term refers to the fact that such individuals are obsessed with some thought or fear or belief and compelled by it to perform a particular action.) Typical behavior includes hoarding string or old newspapers, repeatedly checking doors or appliances to the point of spending hours just trying to leave the house, mentally reciting number patterns over and over, or repeating every single daily routine at least twice. Some rituals are gestural, as was the case with Samuel Johnson, a gifted 18th-century British man of letters who displayed obsessive-compulsive symptoms. A contemporary recounted that every time Johnson passed through a door, he "whirled and twisted about to perform his gesticulations; he would give a sudden spring and make such an extensive stride over the threshold as if he were trying for a wager how far he could stride."

In one exceptionally severe case, reported in 1989 by Dr. Michael Jenike of Massachusetts General Hospital, a woman spent as much as 13 hours a day washing her hands and her house. "Before she could use the soap," recounted Jenike, "she had to use some bleach on the soap to make sure the soap was clean. Before that, she had to use Ajax on the bleach bottle. If she happened to bump the edge of the sink while she was doing this, it would set off another hour and a half, two hours of ritual. She didn't really think there were germs there. It was just a feeling."

The difference emphasized by researchers is that victims of obsessive-compulsive disorder are usually aware that their behavior is irrational, while those with the personality disorder have, in a sense, incorporated their obsessions into their very sense of self. The ritual hand washer, for example, might in other ways come across as a relatively normal person, deeply troubled by her bizarre actions but in some ways detached from them. However, someone afflicted with the personality disorder would be through and through a paragon of fastidiousness, perhaps bothered only by the great effort it takes to keep everyone and everything in line.

Passive-aggressive disorder involves a deeply ingrained resistance to the demands of others, a resistance expressed through indirect methods such as procrastination, stubbornness, sulkiness, and intentional slowness. (The disorder's name refers to behavior that is a passive form of aggression.) Often resentful, critical, and pessimistic, passive-aggressives are exceedingly adept—if unconsciously so—at sabotaging tasks without incurring blame. As one psychologist puts it, they "are invariably an hour late, a dollar short, and a block away, armed with an endless list of excuses to deflect responsibility." They revel in the thrill of insubordination, unaware that their behavior causes their difficulties.

The case of Howard is representative. At first, he seemed like a blessing to his boss at a U.S. accounting firm. Anytime there was extra work to do, Howard volunteered. But soon the boss noticed that Howard was turning in reports late, doing sloppy audits, and taking two-hour lunch breaks. When the lapses were pointed out to him, Howard got mad: "I don't have time for this—I've got a ton of work.

Behind the Scenes of an Uncontrollable Urge

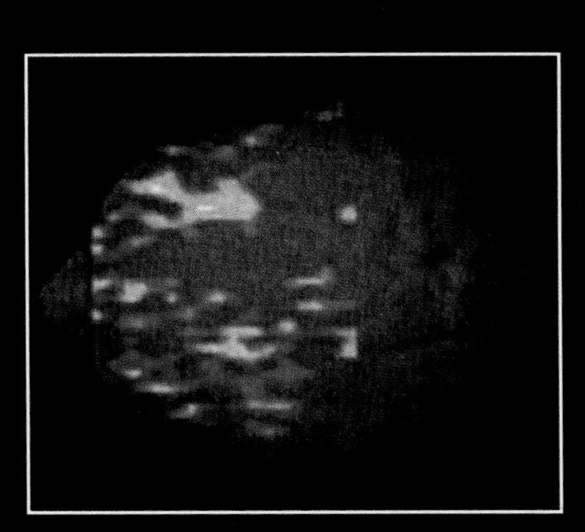

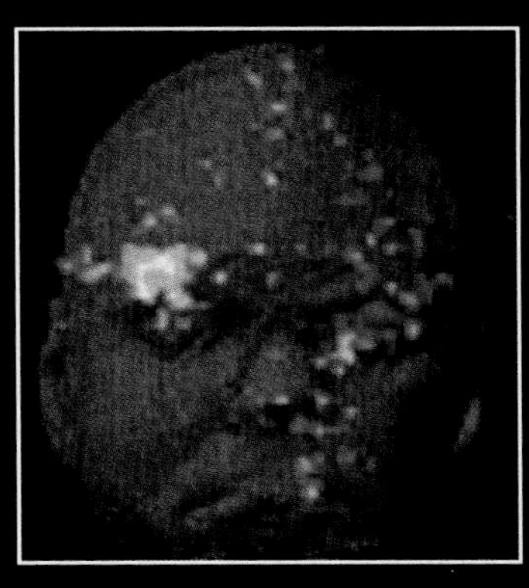

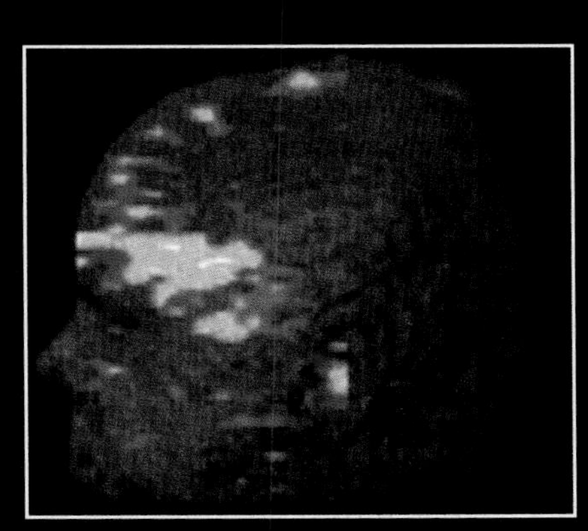

Using new brain-scanning techniques, researchers have been able to take a keener look at the physiological processes underlying obsessive-compulsive disorder, a disease whose meaningless rituals—such as repeatedly checking the lock on a door—rule the lives of its victims. One method involves a fast type of magnetic resonance imaging (MRI) known as echo-planar MRI, which created the three-dimensional images above by combining 80 two-dimensional scans taken every three seconds.

The pattern of brain activity revealed in these views marks the precise moment when a person suffering from obsessive-compulsive disorder was shown an envelope soiled with illicit drugs. Although such an envelope might raise a sense of mild revulsion in many, this patient reacted with an intense need to wash his hands.

The bright patch of yellow just behind the subject's right eye indicates heightened activity in a section of the frontal cortex, a part of the brain that coordinates emotion and thought with behavior. Although the complex biological causes of obsessive-compulsive disorder have yet to be fully understood, researchers believe that this area of the brain plays a key role.

I'm doing the work of three people!"

Outside the workplace, the same patterns prevail. People with the disorder continually misconstrue personal relationships as struggles in which they are powerless. But passive-aggressives are virtually never confrontational or assertive. If they are asked by their spouse to complete a chore or arrive at a social function on time, they use tactics such as forgetfulness or lateness to spoil the event. They also manipulate others into performing errands for them and handling their routine duties. Almost invariably, such behavior creates resentment and anger, but for passive-aggressives, the fault is always with the other person. Left untreated, the situation rarely improves: Accompanying problems of passive-aggressive disorder include major depression and alcohol abuse.

Avoidant disorder entails great social discomfort and an extreme sensitivity to rejection. Sufferers shy away from jobs that require substantial contact with other people, and they have few close friends or confidants outside their own family. Conversations are often painful and awkward. People with the disorder are typically very self-effacing and uncertain and at the same time terrified that they will betray their inner feelings by blushing or crying or simply being unable to answer a question. They cherish the familiar and fear anything beyond the customary routines of life. To avoid situations that stir anxiety, they will invent excuses. They may cancel a trip on the unlikely grounds that rain might make driving dangerous, or they may plead exhaustion to escape going to a party. Sometimes they have specific phobias, and they often suffer from depression, anxiety, and feelings of anger at themselves.

Dependent disorder also involves an extreme lack of self-confidence, but the chief mode of expression is a pattern of submissive and dependent behavior. A person with the disorder often cannot make the smallest decision without advice and support from others. A husband may constantly look to his wife for decisions on where to live or work and who should be included in their circle of friends. Although dependent individuals find it hard to initiate projects, they often seek approval by volunteering for jobs regarded as unpleasant or demeaning. Typically, sufferers hate to be alone. They harbor deep fears of abandonment and are shattered when relationships end. As with most of the other anxiety-based disorders, depression is a frequent complication.

Emotional, overly dramatic, or erratic behavior characterizes a second cluster of personality disorders.

Histrionic disorder manifests itself in repeated instances of theatricality and attention seeking. People with this disorder tend to be extremely self-centered, with a bottomless need for reassurance and praise. By the same token, they are uneasy in situations where they cannot seize the spotlight. Histrionics place great importance on their physical and sexual attractiveness, often to the point of appearing inappropriately seductive. They draw attention to themselves by their liveliness, flamboyance, and over-the-top reactions. They may sob uncontrollably at something most people would find merely sad, or give way to peals of laughter when others would be only mildly amused. Tears and tantrums are common. Their manner of speech tends to be long on feeling but short on details. Asked to describe a vacation, a histrionic person may effuse, "Absolutely fantastic!"—yet be unable to say why. They tell stories that, to listeners, have a cardboard, melodramatic quality.

The relationships of histrionic persons are mostly superficial and short-lived, because the sufferers drive people away with their vanity, inconsistency, and dependence. Their flirtatiousness sometimes conceals sexual problems, including impotence. As they grow older, some histrionics become highly promiscuous or develop a drug habit, and they may get into trouble with the law. Studies of prison populations have found that histrionic personality disorder is common among female inmates. No matter what the course of their life, they are rarely able to explain their motivations and are generally unaware of their real feelings.

Narcissistic disorder draws its name from the Greek tale of Narcissus, a handsome youth who was loved by a wood nymph but became so infatuated with his own reflection in a pool that he ignored her; the nymph retaliated by transforming him into a flower that was doomed to droop over the pool forever, seeing only itself. It is closely related to histrionic behavior but with some notable differences. Like histrionics, narcissists are often preoccupied with grooming or maintaining a youthful appearance, and they may fake emotions or act them out in dramatic ways to impress others. More so than histrionic individuals, people with a narcissistic personality have a grandiose sense of self-importance that, to them, is quite real and overarching. They tend to be more deeply disturbed than histrionics and icier in their dealings with others. Narcissists behave as if they are entitled to favorable treatment or deference wherever they go. Typically, they will cut to the front of a long line, ignoring with complete indifference the protests of those behind them. They refuse to recognize or identify with the feelings of others—even parents, spouses, or children.

Inevitably, their relationships are troubled. The mother of a woman named Abby is a case in point. The daughter discovered a lump in her breast while her mother was visiting her in New York. Abby's doctor offered her an appointment the very next day, when she had planned to attend a theater matinée with her mother. Her mother reacted with irritation, saying, "You always find some reason to get out of spending time with me when I'm here. What difference would one more day make?" Abby's lump turned out to be benign, but the comment added another invisible scar to the many she already bore as a result of her parent's narcissism.

A psychoanalyst familiar with many such examples defines the uncontrolled narcissist as "a person with a two-year-old's self-absorption and demands walking around in the body of an adult." On occasion the disorder appears along with much more serious mental disturbances. A number of serial killers—among them Ted Bundy, who brutally murdered some 36 young women—have been diagnosed as pathological narcissists: Their victims are no more than objects, existing only to satisfy their needs.

Antisocial disorder, as the name suggests, is characterized by a refusal to accept social norms, and some of its symptoms—including cruelty to animals and setting fires—become evident early in life, before the age of 15 and sometimes much sooner. It affects about three times as many males as females, a discrepancy that has yet to be explained either in terms of differing social pressures on girls and boys or by some kind of biological bias. The disorder often first reveals itself in a general belligerent attitude and in episodes of stealing, lying, vandalism, and truancy, accompanied by noticeable absence of remorse. Characteristic behaviors in adulthood include promiscuity, spouse or child abuse, reckless driving, and a wide range of criminal activities. Often, people with the disorder show no interest in holding a job and instead travel aimlessly from place to place, rarely planning ahead. They ignore their debts and also tend to express little concern for the welfare of their children. Frequently, they abuse drugs or alcohol, and many are destined to spend years in prison. Their chances of dying an early and violent death are much higher than among the general population.

Borderline disorder is so named because it represents a kind of crossover condition between neurosis (a generalized state of anxiety) and psychosis (a more severe emotional or mental illness). Its principal feature is an extremely high degree of instability in self-image, emotions, relationships, and overall behavior. The disorder is among the most difficult to diagnose, because it is often combined with symptoms of narcissistic, histrionic, and antisocial disorders among others. But borderline individuals—twice as many females as males—are distinctively unmoored from an emotional center.

The case of one attractive young woman named Mary is illustrative. At a favorite restaurant, she gave the maître d'hôtel a handsome tip for his generous attention one week, but on her next visit she slapped him and burst into tears after being told that she would have to wait for a table. On another occasion, after making passionate love with her boyfriend, she tearfully threatened to slit her wrists if he left the bed.

People with the disorder have rapid mood swings, growing very anxious at times or plunging into a deep depression that lasts for only a few hours. They have difficulty controlling their anger and tend to get into fights or to vent their rage in verbal outbursts. Their sense of identity is unclear: They may be uncertain about their sexual orientation, their preferred values, or their long-term goals.

Impulsiveness, often with a self-destructive component, is a common attribute. Borderline individuals may, for example, go on shopping sprees they clearly cannot afford, indulge in binge eating, take wild drives, shoplift, turn to drugs, or search for casual sex. Sometimes the self-damaging urge is direct and explicit: Sufferers may not only threaten suicide but, to prove they mean it, scratch their wrists or mutilate themselves in some other way. At times of great stress, exaggerated emotions give way to a profound sense of numbness and emptiness. During such moments, a borderline person cannot bear to be alone and, in a pinch, will accept anyone as a companion, even a complete stranger.

The disorder sometimes leads its victims to commit desperate acts. Dr. Rif El-Mallakh of the University of Louisville School of Medicine in Kentucky has noted one particularly extreme case. The patient was a 45-year-old lab technologist who continually injected herself with hazardous hospital wastes. She had been troubled for many years by psychiatric problems ranging from impulsive behavior and anxiety to outbursts of violence and several attempts at suicide—all of which fit with a diagnosis of borderline personality disorder. At a clinic in Washington, D.C., where El-Mallakh first saw her, the patient was treated with perphenazine, an antidepressant. The drug seemed to help, but after discharge, the woman reverted to her former ways. Obtaining a job as a hospital-based medical technologist, she injected herself 20 times with serum containing HIV, the virus that causes AIDS. Later, she told doctors that this relieved her inner turmoil and gave her a soothing sense of control over her life. She eventually contracted AIDS, made four more suicide attempts, and was rehospitalized.

A third and last cluster encompasses disorders characterized by odd and eccentric behavior.

Schizoid disorder features a marked indifference to social relationships, a pattern of isolation and introversion, and a very narrow emotional life. A typical case is that of Joe, who in his accounting job never displayed any feelings, remaining immersed in his numbers and often mumbling to himself. His home life consisted of a rigid routine of reading newspapers and watching television. He had no personal attachments and no evident desire for them. After a colleague took over some of his responsibilities, Joe had great difficulty adapting to new routines and constantly complained in flat tones that he needed to adhere to his "way of doing things." He sought psychiatric counseling only at the insistence of a co-worker.

According to estimates, as many as one person in 12—more men than women—may suffer from schizoid disorder. Most choose solitary jobs, and many prefer night work. They are classic loners: distant, withdrawn, and generally noncompetitive. Their sex life is minimal and often limited to

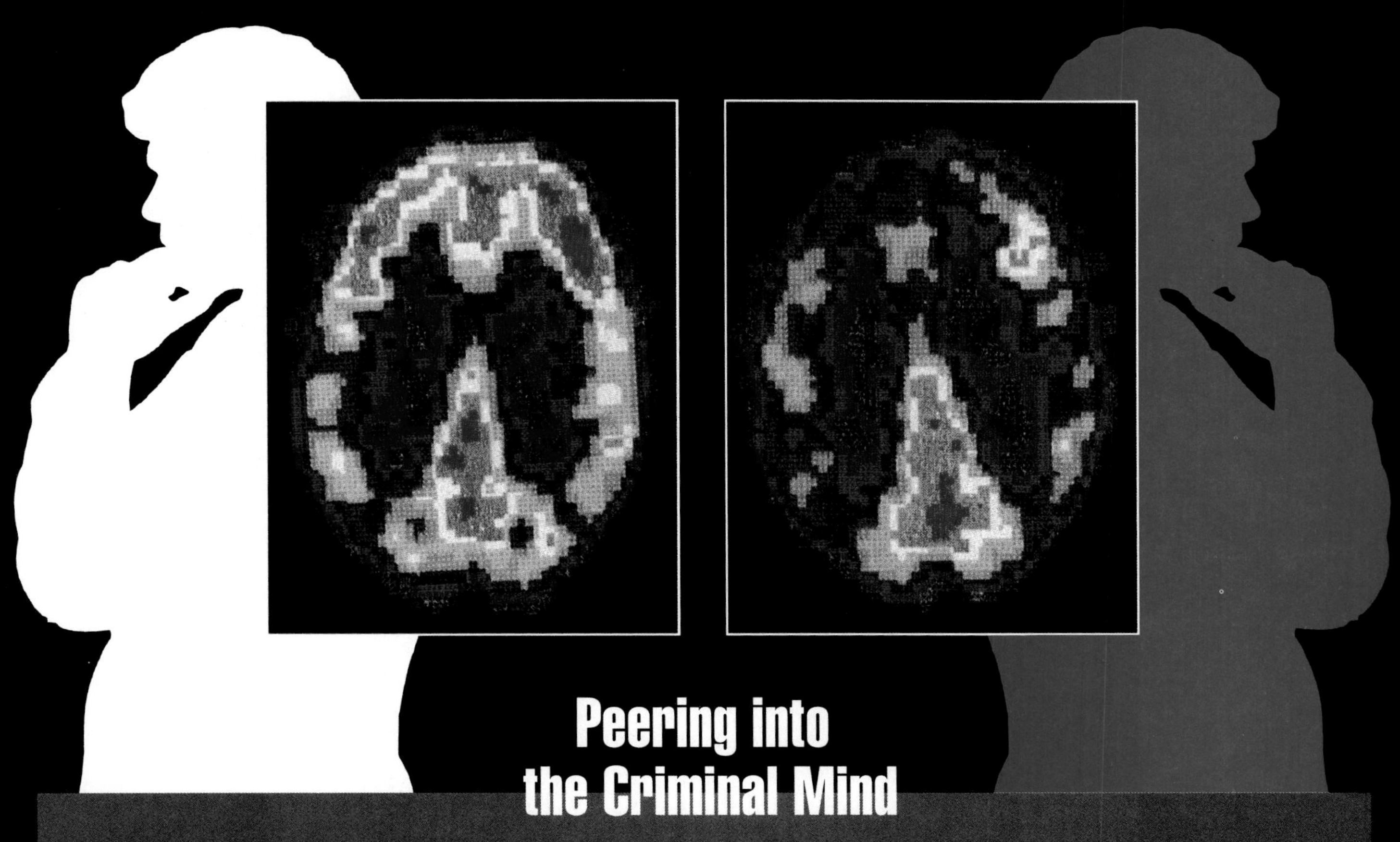

Peering into the Criminal Mind

The search for the roots of deviant behavior has taken some strange turns. One of the oddest was the 19th-century "science" of phrenology, whose practitioners claimed the ability to discern personality traits—including a bent toward lawlessness—from patterns of bumps on the skull. Although this notion has since been debunked, modern research does indicate links between brain physiology and criminal behavior. Studies have shown, for example, that reduced functioning in certain regions of the brain occurs more frequently among some types of criminals than in the general population.

PET scans of two brains—that of a murderer (*above, right*) and that of a noncriminal (*left*)—reveal significant differences in the prefrontal cortex, the portion of the brain that lies immediately behind the forehead. Red and yellow blotches at the top of the noncriminal's scan represent normal levels of metabolic activity. But the predominance of blue in the murderer's scan indicates lower activity, a sign of reduced information processing. Researchers have determined that such deficits of prefrontal activity occur at a higher-than-average rate in violent criminals, child assaulters, and sex offenders.

These criminals also commonly exhibit reduced activity in the frontal lobe, the cortical region just behind the prefrontal lobe that serves as the center for higher thought processes such as planning. A deficit in this part of the brain may lead to increased impulsiveness, loss of self-control, immaturity, and poor social judgment—often a recipe for violence.

None of these discoveries, of course, proves that reduced brain activity causes criminal behavior. At most, such physiological differences produce only a predisposition to criminality, to which few individuals actually succumb. Indeed, further studies may reveal that brain dysfunction is not a cause at all but merely another symptom, and that both the behavior and mental activity of criminals are influenced by other factors, unknown and perhaps unknowable.

fantasizing. In social situations they are quiet, and they have great difficulty expressing anger directly. Some devote all of their energy to mathematics, astronomy, and other studies rich in abstractions. Some become deeply committed to health fads and dietary schemes but usually in a way that requires minimal human involvement. They do not care about the praise or criticism of others, nor do they respond to friendly approaches. Their overriding desire is to be left alone.

Schizotypal disorder shows itself in odd beliefs—idiosyncratic superstitions, for example, or a sense of having mind-reading powers—and a fixation on all things mystical and magical. People with this disorder may claim an ability to discern hidden patterns in the cosmos or detect forces that are unrecognized by others. "I feel an evil presence in the room," they might say, or perhaps announce that other people are listening in on their thoughts. They typically develop elaborate fantasy worlds revolving around imaginary relationships and bizarre fears.

The social life of schizotypal individuals is very limited. Usually, they have no close friends except perhaps family members, and they are uncom-

Who's Responsible When One Self Kills?

Wanda Weston (*above*) is a classic example of an antisocial personality. Her criminal record includes forgery, armed robbery, and the 1979 murder of an elderly woman. Her case, however, is far from typical: Weston is but one of eight personalities sharing the body of a law-abiding Florida woman named Juanita Maxwell. Insisting that she had no control over Wanda's actions, Maxwell became the first person in the state's history to be found not guilty of a crime by reason of insanity because she has multiple personality disorder (*pages* 93-99).

Since the late 1970s, a growing number of Americans faced with criminal charges have claimed to have this disorder, maintaining that alter personalities were responsible for their crimes. Although courts have recognized some of these defendants as legitimate victims of the condition, others have been suspected of fabricating alter personalities in order to plead insanity and avoid the most extreme penalties. Kenneth Bianchi, for example, one of the infamous Hillside Stranglers, initially fooled a number of experts. Eventually, however, his lack of prior amnesiac episodes and the overly dramatic and inconsistent presentation of his supposed alters revealed him to have only one personality: that of a clever sociopath. He was sentenced to life in prison in 1979.

fortable with strangers. Their speech tends to be jumpy, vague, and abstract, and their mannerisms may be inappropriate and silly. They do not return smiles or respond to friendly gestures. A slipshod appearance is also common. For them the only meaningful world is within, and they often talk to themselves.

Schizotypal disorder afflicts an estimated three percent of the population. Some researchers think it is a kind of muted schizophrenia, the much more devastating mental illness with which it shares a number of symptoms. Schizophrenia, which usually strikes in adolescence or early adulthood, is a delusional, reality-fracturing disease: Victims suddenly begin sleeping at odd hours and withdrawing to their room or a private place in the attic or basement. They whisper to invisible companions, talk back to the television set, or violently try to shoo away spirits or demons. They become paralyzed by irrational fears, sometimes insisting that their thoughts are being monitored by the CIA or by aliens from outer space, and they may surrender the self altogether, claiming that their body is occupied by some long-dead historical figure such as Napoleon.

At times of great stress, a person with schizotypal disorder may experience a schizophrenia-like psychotic break with reality—but only briefly. Many sufferers are able to live relatively stable lives. For some, however, the disorder is ultimately unbearable. According to one estimate, 10 percent of those suffering from the disorder eventually commit suicide.

Paranoid disorder is characterized by a persistent, unjustified mistrust of others and a tendency to react to perceived slights or threats with anger or even violence. Such people are emotionally aloof and tense, openly disdainful of weakness in others, and rigidly insistent on having their own way. The idea of compromise is alien to them; they are deeply afraid of losing control over their life or being unable to shape events according to their wishes. At the same time, they are very conscious of rank and jealous of those whom they see as holding power in society or in an organization. Often they interpret the actions of other people as deliberately demeaning or threatening, and they will bear grudges for years, passionately avoiding blame for a fight even if the blame is entirely warranted. Although individuals with paranoid personality disorder rarely function well in social situations, they may perform quite well at jobs in which they do not have to cooperate with fellow workers.

Some people with the disorder may, because of gifts of energy and intelligence, gain the sort of absolute power and control they crave, but it almost never lasts. Cult leaders such as David Koresh (*page* 83) or the murderous Charles Manson epitomize the dark potential of the breed. Their need to dominate and their conviction of the world's hostility are classic symptoms of paranoid disorder (although Manson most likely also suffers from more severe mental illnesses such as schizophrenia). They presented themselves as messiahs, spinning out visions of apocalyptic events that would lend meaning to the lives of their followers—mostly outsiders who had given up on ordinary society and wanted to relinquish all responsibility to someone who would control them.

Paranoid disorder may predispose its victims to the more extreme condition of paranoid schizophrenia, which can cause individuals to seek what the charismatic Jim Jones, leader of a cult known as the Peoples Temple, called "the orgasm of the grave." In the Temple's jungle compound of Jonestown in the South American country of Guyana, he took more than 900 people to the grave with him.

Jim Jones is one of recent history's

Adherents and adversaries remarked on the extraordinary power in the gaze of David Koresh *(right),* pictured here in Waco, Texas, three months before he led his sect to fiery destruction in 1993.

A crowd in Simla, India, parts to make way for Indian nationalist Mahatma Gandhi. In contrast to the enormous fervor surrounding him, Gandhi himself *(below)* usually radiated serenity.

The Persuasive Power of Charisma

tions could scarcely have been more dif-
ndhi, the Indian nationalist whose non-
is nation to independence, and David Ko-
d gun-wielding prophet of an ill-fated
co, Texas. Even so, Gandhi and Koresh
ystical quality known as charisma, and on
personal magnetism they built movements
ation and obedience of their followers.
m the Greek meaning a "gift of grace,"
d movie-star glamour or mere physical
xperts are hard-pressed to define exactly
it comes from. Charismatic individuals
tain personality traits, including aggres-
and the ability to arouse emotion. Excep-
er; not all charismatic individuals are ag-
stic, for instance, and in a great many
tion of these characteristics fails to light
e.

el the secret of charisma lies in certain
a mesmerizing voice, perhaps, or a pene-
researchers probe deeper in an effort to
ic, they have learned that much of cha-
de in the eyes of its beholders. Figures such as Gandhi and Koresh often emerge in times of trouble, fulfilling the needs of people in search of a savior. Those who become followers tend to be psychologically dependent, either by their very nature or as a result of severe stress. Over long periods, stress can create a sense of despair and loss of control, leading to a willingness to turn over decision making to someone with an aura of strength and knowledge.

Anthropologist Charles Lindholm suggests that charisma is not so much a trait, existing on its own, as it is a relationship, a phenomenon that "appears only in interaction with others who lack it." Generally the relationship is one-sided: Although inspiring passion among followers and greatly influencing their behavior—perhaps even provoking them to kill others or themselves—a charismatic leader typically seems to remain unswayed by the followers' actions.

Whatever its origin, charisma is clearly a double-edged sword, working either as a positive force or as an extremely destructive one. The same intensity of spirit that made a hero of Mahatma Gandhi also sparked fanatical enthusiasm for the likes of David Koresh, Charles Manson, and Adolf Hitler. "Apparently," write the editors of a 1986 work on the subject, "charismatic leaders may be possessed of the gift of the devil as well as the gift of grace."

most horrifying demonstrations of how a personality disorder can tighten its hold over a period of years and ultimately devour the sufferer. Born in Indiana in 1931, Jones had a miserable childhood. His father, a cold and embittered invalid, died when Jones was young. His mother was also troubled. She had enjoyed a more privileged upbringing than her husband and fancied herself an exceptional person, but she ended up working in a factory, consoling herself with alcohol. She paid little attention to her son. He later said, "I was ready to kill by the end of the third grade. Nobody gave me any love, any understanding. I'm standing there. Alone. Always alone."

He was, however, unmistakably special. Even as a boy, he proved himself a master manipulator of people's emotions, a talent he first displayed in revivalist meetings held by the local Pentecostal church, where he earned a reputation as a budding child evangelist. The meetings afforded some release of his inner tension, but he gave them up, believing that they exacerbated the insomnia and nightmares that had begun to plague him. He did not give up manipulating people, however. At home, he staged theatrical performances for friends, orating, portraying himself as someone with the power to heal, weaving fantasies of omnipotence and death.

As a teenager, he took up preaching again, hitchhiking to the larger towns in Indiana and seeking out audiences on the streets and frequently in African American communities. Jones went on to college, married, and held a series of jobs, but success and satisfaction eluded him until he found a way to re-create the environment of total control he had enjoyed in his theatricals at home. The method he settled on was to organize his own Pentecostal church, the Peoples Temple. From the start, he was a dictator—tireless, brilliantly eloquent, always available to comfort or counsel his parishioners, but a dictator nonetheless. In effect, he required his followers to give up their lives to the Temple. They had to surrender all their assets. (As it turned out, most of his followers came from backgrounds of extreme poverty but still managed in their numbers to provide a surprising amount of wealth for the Temple.) And they had to participate in endless, emotionally charged services featuring public confessions of their own deep flaws, accompanied by fervent affirmations of the infinite wisdom of their leader. In sermons, Jones told his flock that he would bring about a social revolution based on interracial harmony and communal values. But he confided that he was much more than a political and ethical genius. He was also God—the Supreme Being incarnate.

Jim Jones was an extremely watchful and suspicious God, however. He said that society wanted to prevent his revolution and that the Temple was in danger of nuclear destruction. He knew about the dangers, he explained, because he had received extraterrestrial messages. He also claimed that guns had already been used against members of the Temple. These shooting incidents may have been real, but if so, they were no doubt carried out by Jones himself to convince his followers that the Peoples Temple was under siege.

In early 1962, Jones had a mental breakdown and decamped to Brazil. Two years later he returned, resumed his control of the Peoples Temple in Indiana, then shifted his base of operations to California. There, he demonstrated more skill than ever in eliciting wild emotional responses with his sermonizing and in maneuvering others into a position of dependence through forced orgies of self-criticism. He devised a rigid command structure for the Temple, created a thicket of rules (which he often changed on a whim), and refined his stagecraft with such touches as preaching from a thronelike chair that was flanked by an American flag and a framed copy

A leader with truly horrific powers of persuasion, Jim Jones lured some 900 cult followers to drink a lethal fruit-flavored potion that was laced with cyanide and sedatives *(above)*. Jones had earlier conducted trial runs of this mass "revolutionary suicide."

Boundaries Thick and Thin

While studying nightmare sufferers, psychiatrist Ernest Hartmann of Tufts University was struck by the similarities in personality among his subjects. Exceedingly creative and imaginative, they tended to be vulnerable, open, and highly sensitive to both physical and emotional pain. Based on these findings, he formulated a new theory of personality.

The nightmare sufferers, Hartmann concluded, were people with "thin boundaries." That is, the barriers in their lives—between thoughts and feelings, between themselves and others, between reality and fantasy—were exceptionally delicate and easily breached. Hartmann has also found people with what he describes as very thick boundaries. Logical, inflexible, and guarded, such people see the world in black and white, with little room for gray. These differences may have their basis in the organization of the brain. Hartmann's preliminary research suggests that people with thin boundaries may have more intricate connections among neurons in the cortex.

Inordinate thickness or thinness of boundaries seems to be the exception rather than the norm. A so-called boundary questionnaire administered by Hartmann to more than 2,000 subjects appears to show that most people—among whom Hartmann includes himself—occupy a middle ground.

of the Declaration of Independence. At its high point, the Temple had more than 5,000 members. When politicians became aware of the hold he had on his following and his supposed program of love and harmony, they helped install him in a city commission job in San Francisco.

Indeed, love was the Temple's banner, its avowed reason for being. But love in the context established by Jones meant nothing more or less than worship of Jim Jones: He was the embodiment and the wellspring of love. Members were required to use the salutation "Jim loves you" whenever they met. He taught that family love was a snare and a delusion. As one member of the Peoples Temple put it, "The church is your family now. Families are part of the enemy system."

In his desire to eradicate normal family ties, Jones took control of the sex lives of his devotees. He assigned new partners to married couples, making selections designed to ensure minimal mutual attraction. Sometimes he insisted that his followers be celibate, saying that "the only reason sex would ever become necessary would be to produce children, and of course at this time in history, when we are concerned about an impending nuclear disaster, we don't need any babies in the group." He, of course, was the exception, the ultimate progenitor and lover. Sex with him was transcendence, a fusion with the Divine, a dissolving of the self in his greatness.

Jones was an extraordinarily vigorous man and hardly slept at all, at least in part because of an addiction to amphetamines. He devoted countless hours to satisfying his own sexual appetites, which were homosexual as well as heterosexual. (At one point, he was arrested for homosexual solicitation in a public men's room.) For him, sex was always an act of domination, intended to prove the powerlessness of others. With female parishioners, he cultivated an image of sexual superman and often would describe his encounters in detail to the entire congregation. But godlike sexuality was only one of many superhuman attributes he claimed. He also said that he could cure any disease, foresee the future, and read people's minds. Still, being God was a tiring business. He frequently told his flock how worn down he was by his responsibilities.

More and more, Jones saw the world as teeming with enemies. Since dangers were everywhere, he could not tolerate the slightest challenge to his power. The worst threat of all was for someone to leave the Peoples Temple—which began to happen with increasing regularity. Finally, in 1977, he decided upon a policy of retreat. He ordered some of his followers to go to Guyana and construct a refuge beyond the reach of all enemies.

Backed by the large financial resources of the Peoples Temple, these pioneers dutifully established the foundations of an agricultural commune in the jungle. Its name, naturally, was Jonestown. Meanwhile, Jones took steps to persuade other Temple members to join the exodus. They were on a secret CIA list of enemies of the state, he claimed, and if they remained in California would be put in concentration camps and killed. Many believed him. He himself arrived in Jonestown in August of 1977 but once there paid little attention to farming and other practical issues. Instead, he redoubled his efforts to stir the fears of his parishioners and to get them to submerge their identity in his.

But Guyana was not far enough away. On November 14, 1978, Congressman Leo Ryan of California arrived with staff members, journalists, and relatives of Jonestown residents to investigate reports of the tyrannical regime Jones had set up. Jones grew deeply depressed when he learned that many of his people wanted to return to the United States with Ryan, and he finally ordered the congressman killed. Some of his followers did the job on the 17th, ambushing Ryan and gunning him down along with four others. Several members of Ryan's party did escape, and at that point Jones decided that the Peoples Temple was doomed to fall to its enemies.

On the loudspeaker system of the compound, he began talking about "the beauty of dying" and the certainty that everyone would meet again "in another place." The road to death had, in fact, already been prepared. On Jones's instructions, the camp doctor produced a vat of artificially flavored fruit drink mixed with cyanide. The doctor and nurses began dispensing it to the assembly, starting with the children. Some people had last-minute doubts and tried to get away, but they were restrained by guards. In the end, almost everyone followed their leader on this last journey. Jones, being special, apparently chose a shortcut. He was found shot in the head.

According to the view of some psychiatrists, Jim Jones was not by definition a madman. His life was ruled by a set of needs and a way of thinking that, while warped and destructive, may have fallen short of true mental illness. He could function in society, and in some ways he functioned spectacularly well. Yet something had gone profoundly wrong with his personality.

Just why this happens to certain people and not to others is, of course, one of the oldest and most important problems faced by psychiatrists and mental-health workers. One certainty is that, as with all aspects of human development, personality disorders result from an interaction between genes and environment. A psychotherapist might make much of Jim Jones's distant, unhappy father and his early death, not to mention Jones's unloving, hard-drinking mother. But no one knows whether these factors in his childhood environment were the principal determinants of his paranoid personality, or if some genetic predisposition was the chief reason the disorder fastened itself so tightly on him. In fact, the relative importance of genetic endowment and environment is unclear for most personality disorders.

Researchers have accumulated

some suggestive evidence, however. When Dr. Michael Stone of Columbia College of Physicians and Surgeons in New York City studied the life histories of female borderline-disorder patients, he spotted what might be an environmental pattern. In some cases, the death of a mother, followed by a father's incestuous advances, had led an adolescent girl to run away and later turn to drug abuse or prostitution. The long downward slide was attended by highly erratic behavior and suicide threats—prime borderline signs.

With certain other disorders, investigations have pointed to a strong genetic component. In the 1960s, for example, a team headed by psychiatrist Seymour Kety of Massachusetts General Hospital initiated an exhaustive study of children of schizophrenic parents adopted by healthy couples. Kety wanted to know if such a child was at greater risk of developing schizophrenia as an adult. Like many other researchers who had studied the mental illness, he found genetic inheritance to be an important risk factor—although being raised in a healthy home environment seemed to lessen the risk. But in the course of years of work and thousands of interviews, Kety and his associates noticed something more subtle: The relatives of schizophrenics tended, as a group, to be a bit strange or odd. They were not schizophrenic but were often quirky, withdrawn, a little random in their thought processes, and prone to believe in magical or supernatural explanations for some of the ways of the world. From Kety's work, psychiatrists constructed diagnoses of a milder condition classified as schizotypal personality disorder.

Biological inheritance also seems to predispose people to the shyness and nervousness seen in avoidant disorder. For example, studies of identical twins reared apart—sharing all of their genes but little in the way of environment—indicate a significant degree of heritability for these traits. Impulsiveness and aggressiveness also emerged from the twins research as apparently inherited traits, suggesting that genes may be an important factor in antisocial disorder as well. A few scientists have tied this and other findings to the controversial issue of criminality. Perhaps crime has a biological basis, they suggest. Perhaps it is not simply a consequence of poverty, a disrupted family life, and other environmental disadvantages.

The idea is an old one, crude in its early versions. In Victorian times, people believed that criminals and sociopaths were more likely to have small, shifty eyes, eyebrows that met

The Good Side of Extremes

To most people, the Chinese student at left was a hero. Standing in the path of a line of tanks during the 1989 student-led uprising in Beijing's Tiananmen Square, he exemplifies the brave defiance of nonviolent resistance. But according to American psychologist Scott Wetzler, the student's behavior, like all acts of civil disobedience, was a form of the same "sugar-coated hostility" exhibited by people with passive-aggressive personality disorder (*pages* 74-76).

This particular disorder is not the only personality extreme that has a healthy counterpart. In fact, many theorists believe that behaviors are to some extent judged by their context. People with personality disorders, in other words, are merely displaying socially unacceptable versions of the same kinds of conduct that may be perfectly legitimate, even admirable, in other settings. One writer has suggested that the term "psychopath," for example—which is typically applied to such deviant individuals as mass murderers—actually refers only to the "unsuccessful" psychopath: The same kind of crafty, manipulative behavior that characterizes such antisocial personalities may also typify an enterprising businessperson.

in the middle, sloping foreheads, jutting chins, and long arms. In the 1930s, several states—with the blessing of the U.S. Supreme Court—undertook mass sterilization programs of convicts to reduce crime in future generations. In the 1960s, tabloids brayed about the dramatic "discovery" that men who carry an XYY chromosome pattern, rather than the normal XY male pattern, were predisposed to becoming violent criminals. No definitive evidence existed, but the debate about possible links between genes and crime remains lively. Psychiatrist Samuel B. Guze of the Washington School of Medicine in St. Louis has said that the worst error is the urge to choose between heredity and environment in explaining criminality. "These views are obviously not incompatible and may, on the contrary, be complementary," he notes.

Part of what distinguishes conditions such as obsessive-compulsive disorder from the less-severe personality disorders is that the former do indeed seem to be more strongly influenced by biology. Psychiatrist Judith Rapoport of the National Institute of Mental Health has suggested that the repetitive hand-washing or door-checking actions of obsessive-

A Life in the Mind

By all accounts, daydreaming is a universal human phenomenon, but for some people, such flights of fancy have an extraordinary vividness that blurs the line between what is real and what is only imaginary. These individuals, known to psychologists as fantasy-prone personalities, feel the sting of nonexistent rain, savor the taste of unearthly fruits, and take mental trips to elaborately realized alien worlds. Many spend up to half of their waking life in such realms, and even mistake memories of their fantasies for those of reality.

Surprisingly, despite the hours of reverie, fantasy-prone individuals are often quite successful in their real lives. For example, one woman, a mother of two, has reported that she spends up to 95 percent of her time in fantasy—yet maintains near-perfect grades in graduate school while also writing articles for academic journals.

Studies indicate that fantasy-prone personalities tend to be creative and are easily hypnotized. As children, many enjoyed music, dance, or drama and also felt close to an adult who encouraged them to use their imagination. But recent evidence suggests that they do not all conform to a single personality type. A subset of fantasy-prone people had a very different childhood, in which they suffered abuse and turned to dream territory as an escape.

Later in life, such individuals may have problems leaving their imaginary lives long enough to focus on reality. But for most of the fantasy-prone, their excursions may actually contribute to mental health—providing a restorative break from the rigors of the everyday world.

compulsive disorder may stem from "behavioral 'subroutines' related to grooming and territoriality programmed into the human brain over the course of evolution." In other words, the basis of the disorder may be inscribed in the neural circuitry. Somehow, she says, those ancient, gene-imposed programs go haywire, as though they are disconnected from parts of the brain that normally supply sensory proof that a particular task such as washing or closing a door has been accomplished and need not be performed again.

Some evidence even suggests that such disorders inhabit particular locales in the brain. One bizarre example is the 1983 case of a 19-year-old Englishman named Tom, who was afflicted with a severe compulsion to shower constantly and to wash his hands more than 50 times a day. Unable to hold a job, he grew so distraught that his mother one day suggested in exasperation that he end his misery by shooting himself. So he did, sticking the barrel of a .22-caliber rifle into his mouth and pulling the trigger. But instead of killing him, the bullet apparently destroyed the portion of Tom's brain responsible for the compulsion—"a one-in-a-million shot," said a neurosurgeon. Tom survived, returned to high school shortly after, became an A student, and went on to an otherwise normal life.

During the 1940s and 1950s, American neurosurgeon Walter Freeman, inspired by research work done in Europe, built a small industry on the notion that mental problems have physical locations in the brain. He said that psychosurgery was the perfect cure for people suffering from emotional difficulties such as severe anxiety. One of his procedures, called a prefrontal lobotomy, involved drilling a hole in the skull and sweeping a blunt knife through brain tissue. Later, for speed and convenience, he merely inserted an ice pick through the eye socket. This technique was known as a "poor man's lobotomy," but it made Freeman plenty of money. He personally performed 3,500 of the operations, usually in his office or the patient's home. The standard charge was $1,000. Unfortunately, a great many of his patients afterward sank into apathy or suffered intellectual impairment as a result of the gross tissue damage of the procedure.

Lobotomies are a thing of the past, but some psychosurgery is still performed. In one procedure, an electrode inserted through a tiny hole drilled in the skull is used to sear a small part of the cingulum, a bundle of nerve fibers linking the emotional and thinking parts of the brain. The operation helps patients suffering from obsessive-compulsive disorder and severe depression, and it does not seem to affect their intellectual abilities or personalities.

As for personality disorders themselves, most treatments based on the notion of a biological origin for the condition are pharmacological rather than surgical. The drugs shown to be effective in alleviating symptoms work by correcting imbalances in neurotransmitters or by mimicking or blocking the effects of these natural brain chemicals. Neurotransmitters released into the synapses linking nerve cells are involved in everything the brain does, from thinking to shutting down for sleep. Although many types of neurotransmitters may be important in personality disorders, the roles of three in particular—dopamine, serotonin, and norepinephrine—have been extensively studied. Dopamine is associated with neural pathways that control emotional stability, among other things. Norepinephrine, in excess, figures in anxiety and fear reactions. Serotonin seems to be ubiquitous in the brain and has been linked to depression and suicidal thoughts, alcohol abuse, panic attacks, and eating disorders. Dealing with neurotransmitters poses considerable pharmacological challenges; serotonin, for example, seems to hitch up with brain cells in more than 20 different ways. But powerful drugs have been developed for the job—among them Prozac (*pages* 106-107) which is routinely prescribed for obsessive-compulsive behavior and has shown effectiveness with some personality disorders.

Some doctors go so far as to view the therapeutic future as primarily pharmacological. Eventually, says one, "every disease is going to be [seen as] a chemical or electrical disease"—personality disorders included. Others regard drugs as little more than a stopgap measure for personality disorders, not a replacement for psychotherapy, or so-called talk therapies that focus on the emotional life of the patient. The fact is that both methods help. Comparative studies indicate that while psychotherapy does not work as quickly as drugs, it appears to catch up in effectiveness after about four months, and it may be more effective in preventing relapses.

Most doctors believe that the best treatment for personality disorders is a blend of the two. Says Dr. Willard Gaylin, director of the Hastings Center in New York: "Anybody who deals with human pain and misery understands there's an interplay, and you use everything available."

A ROOM WITH MANY VIEWS

For ages, people have pondered the mystery of multiple personalities, the rare disorder that allows several "selves" to take up residence in a single body. Some cultures call it spirit possession or proof of demons. Others blame the supernatural or even a failed reincarnation that jumbled several souls into one body. The moving story of a woman named Sybil, told in a 1973 book, generated public interest in multiple personality disorder (MPD), even as skeptics rejected it as nonsense. Not until 1980 did the American Psychiatric Association add MPD as a category in its list of disorders.

Experts define MPD as the existence of two or more contrasting and separate personalities, each determining behavior and attitudes when in control of the body. Because almost all cases seem to be precipitated by childhood trauma, especially sexual abuse and torture, researchers suspect that sufferers involuntarily don different "masks" as a sort of defense mechanism. Whatever its cause, MPD can leave an individual partitioned into dozens of personalities—like a single room with many distinct views.

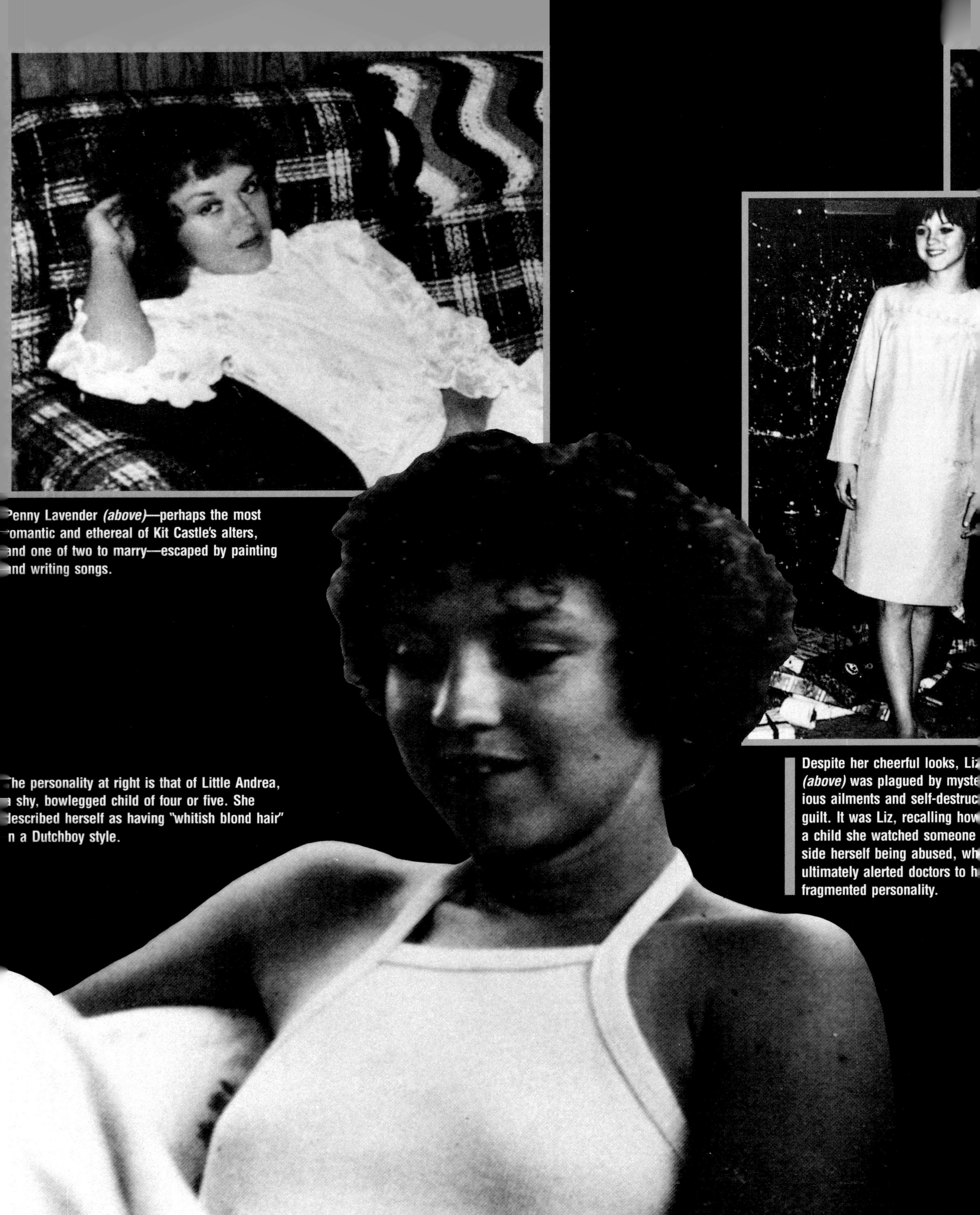

Penny Lavender *(above)*—perhaps the most romantic and ethereal of Kit Castle's alters, and one of two to marry—escaped by painting and writing songs.

The personality at right is that of Little Andrea, a shy, bowlegged child of four or five. She described herself as having "whitish blond hair" in a Dutchboy style.

Despite her cheerful looks, Liz *(above)* was plagued by myste ious ailments and self-destruc guilt. It was Liz, recalling how a child she watched someone side herself being abused, wh ultimately alerted doctors to h fragmented personality.

If the fisherman at left appears to be a little boy, it is because young Jess has come out. Cold and rational, Jess protected his sister personalities when they felt threatened. He dreamed of being a doctor and professed love for Kitty Rosetti *(below)*, unaware they both shared the same body.

Kitty Rosetti *(right)* was a shrewd, tough-minded businesswoman who worked as a stripper. Her painted eyes and dazzling smile won her admirers in clubs from Dallas to Minneapolis, but Kitty, the last major personality to emerge, could be cold and hard.

FRAGMENTS OF A SELF

Liz Castle awoke in a bathtub to find a three-inch surgical scar across her stomach. Horrified, she realized that somehow, without her knowledge, she had undergone a partial hysterectomy. It later became clear that the operation had been performed on Penny Lavender—one of the dozens of personalities who, like Liz, occupied the body of a woman named Kit Castle, some of whose personae appear here.

Life is equally disjointed for many MPD patients. One woman knows who has been "out," or "using the body," only by handwritten messages she finds in a notebook. Each of her adult selves has a unique writing style, and a younger self uses a childish scrawl.

A childlike "alter" is common among people with MPD. When a no-nonsense policeman switches to an impish 10-year-old boy, the change is easily detected by the man's pet dog: Normally banned from the living room, the animal rushes in when the boy comes out to play. In the supermarket, a woman with MPD and her husband watch their two young daughters choose breakfast cereal. Suddenly, the mother becomes a five-year-old with a childlike voice. Soon all three girls are debating which cereal to buy, while the husband waits patiently for his wife to return.

Since the photographs on these pages were taken, Kit Castle's many selves have been fused, through psychotherapy, into one. But for years, her life—like the lives of other MPD patients—was, as she put it, "a basket full of loose pearls, and they were rolling together, mysteriously linking up and then falling apart."

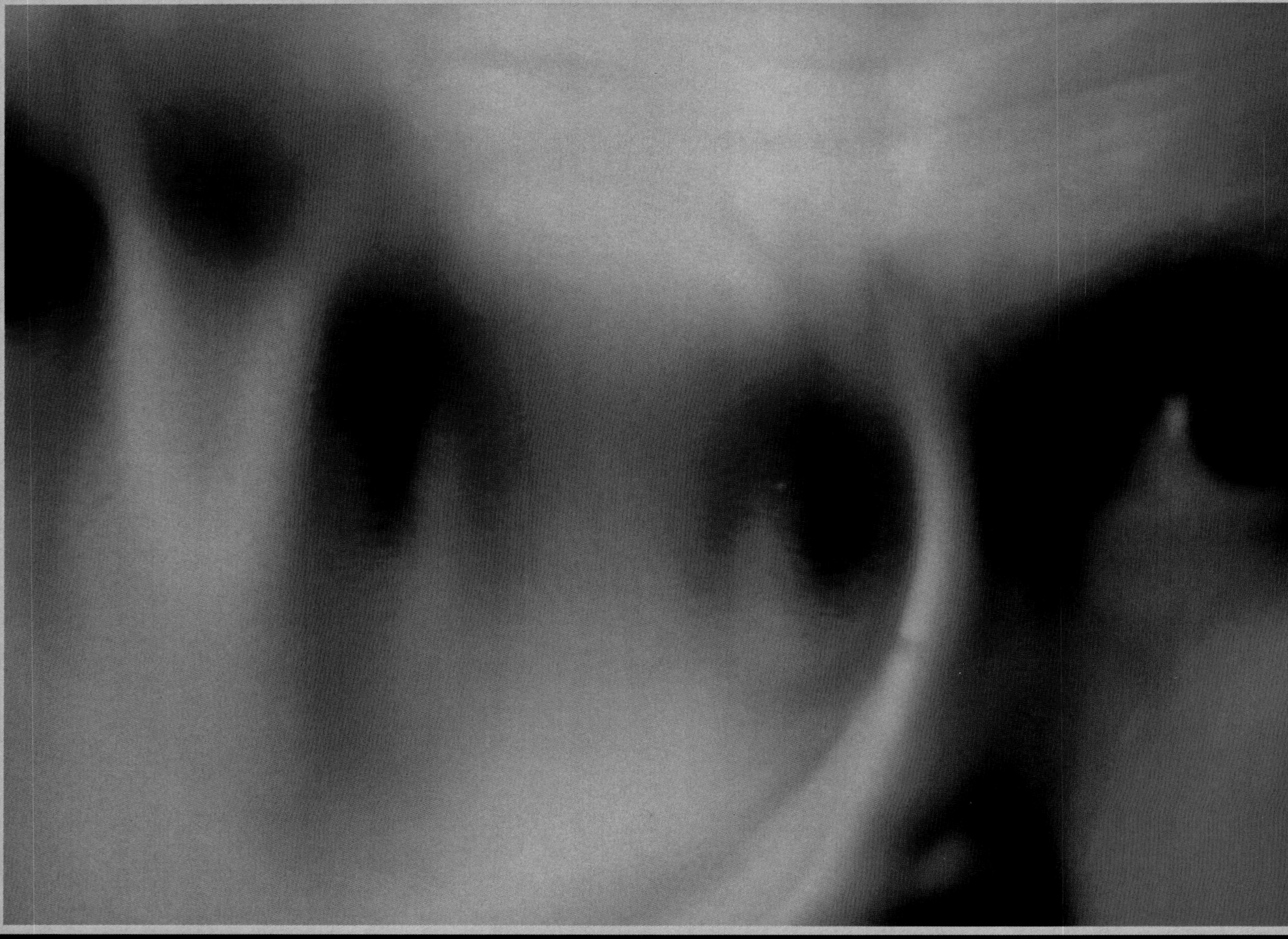

Using an electroencephalograph and electrodes attached to a subject's scalp, researchers can record electrical activity in the brain, then break these signals down into various frequency levels and convert them into colorful graphic "brain maps." The scans at right show the distribution of high-frequency beta 2 waves and low-frequency theta waves in the brains of what look to be three different people. In reality, the maps indicate the beta 2 and theta wave activity of three distinct personalities sharing the body of a woman with multiple personality disorder. In both groups, images labeled Alter A show brain activity recorded when the subject's personality was that of a child. The maps of Alter B were created when an obsessive-compulsive personality had control of the body. Alter C is the subject's host personality. The colors represent degrees of electrical activity, measured in microvolts: Bright red and yellow indicate areas with high-intensity waves; green and blue show regions with low-level brain activity. As researchers have discovered, the brain maps of an MPD patient's myriad selves can be as different from each other as those of individual human beings. However, few scientists care to speculate about how these patterns may be linked to behavior.

NOT JUST A STATE OF MIND

Recent studies showing marked physical differences among an individual's separate "selves" offer some of the most convincing evidence that multiple personality disorder really exists. In some cases, for example, each personality has its own characteristic heart rate or its own set of allergies. Even visual acuity can vary; one personality might have perfect vision while another cannot see without glasses. Sometimes one alter gets tipsy after having too much to drink —and another suffers the hangover.

Brain activity usually varies among the different personalities and stays constant over time, with each self registering its own unique pattern during a series of tests (*below*). Such findings do not necessarily mean that MPD is caused by a brain abnormality or chemical imbalance, although this may be true. Some researchers think MPD may be similar to conditions such as manic-depressive disorder that seem to bring about changes in the body. Curiously, even normal people have been known to change physically under hypnosis or during meditation, switching from being right- to left-handed, for example, or healing at a different rate.

Because many people with MPD are easily hypnotized, researchers have speculated that the alters are products of a self-induced trance. While this notion is widely rejected as inadequate, MPD patients do exhibit a sort of mental partitioning, which probably arises from a phenomenon called state-dependent learning: Each state, or personality, learns or does things that cannot always be recalled by the other states. Again, this phenomenon is not limited to MPD patients. Most people recall events better when they are in a like frame of mind. A man who lost his car keys during a binge, for example, can find them more easily drunk than sober.

Beta 2 Waves

Alter A

Alter B

Alter C

Theta Waves

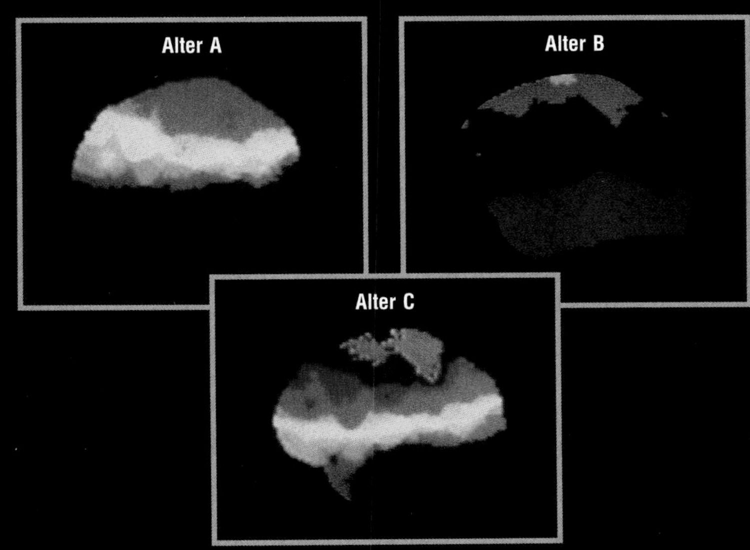

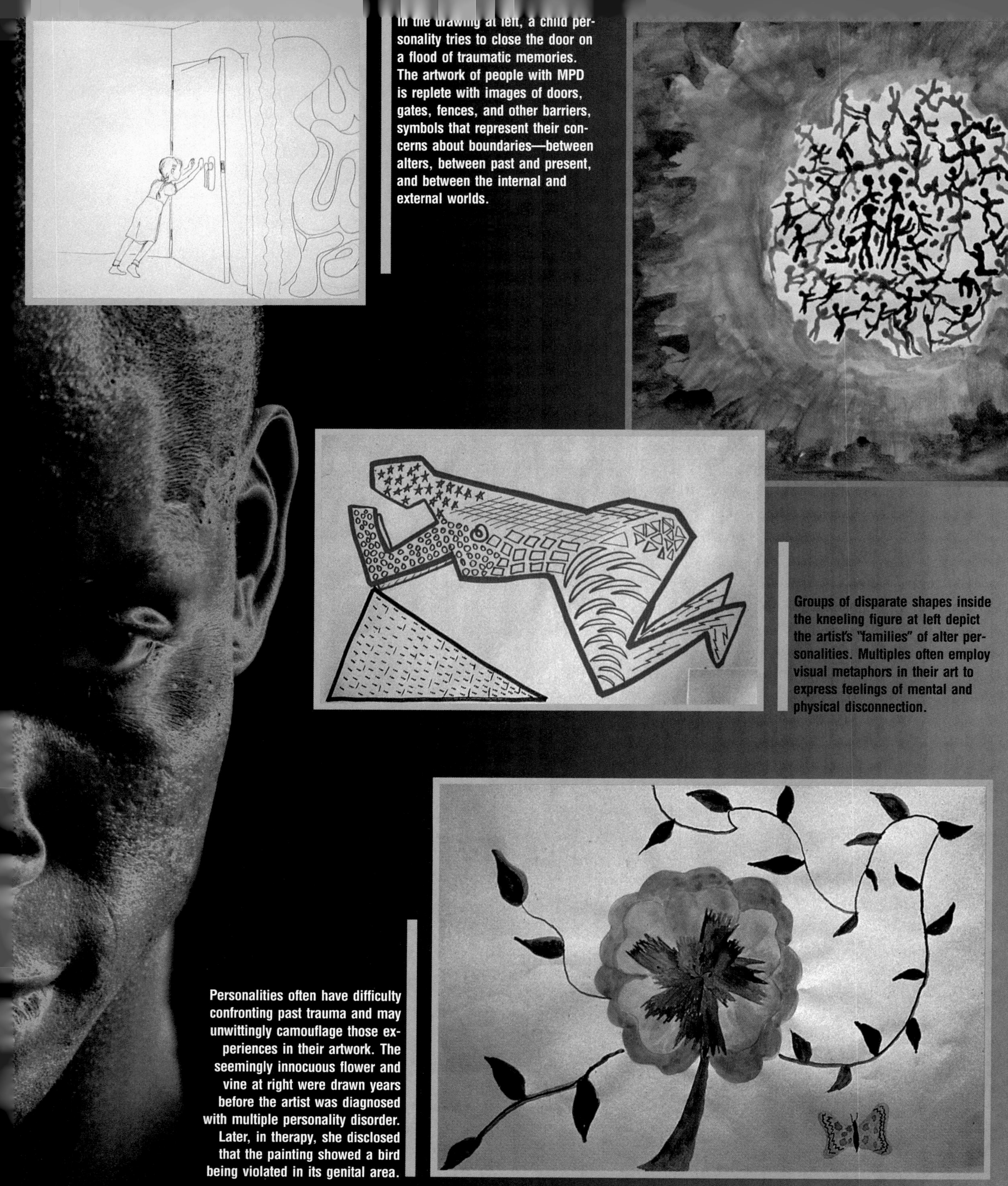

In the drawing at left, a child personality tries to close the door on a flood of traumatic memories. The artwork of people with MPD is replete with images of doors, gates, fences, and other barriers, symbols that represent their concerns about boundaries—between alters, between past and present, and between the internal and external worlds.

Groups of disparate shapes inside the kneeling figure at left depict the artist's "families" of alter personalities. Multiples often employ visual metaphors in their art to express feelings of mental and physical disconnection.

Personalities often have difficulty confronting past trauma and may unwittingly camouflage those experiences in their artwork. The seemingly innocuous flower and vine at right were drawn years before the artist was diagnosed with multiple personality disorder. Later, in therapy, she disclosed that the painting showed a bird being violated in its genital area.

Rings of human figures, many joined at the hands, frolic inside a brightly colored sunflower in the painting at left. Art therapists Barry M. Cohen and Carol Cox, who devised a classification system for MPD artwork, call this type of drawing a system picture because it shows how diverse elements—the artist's alter personalities—work together as a unit.

The three-part image below is a collaborative effort. One personality, working with felt-tip pens, drew the horrific scene on the left, and another used crayons to produce the serene, childlike figures on the right. A third added the "inkblot" in the middle. Such drawings, vividly illustrating the switching process among alters, are the hallmark of MPD art.

In so-called trance drawings, such as the dreamlike sketch below, multiples use images to convey ideas or emotions that defy expression in words. Even the artists frequently admit bewilderment at these pictures, which have been described as "pictorial free association."

BUILDING ONE FROM THE MANY

A fragmented personality can be extremely disruptive. In the words of psychiatrist Bennett Braun, "Any country ruled by committee—like a junta—ends up with a revolution." The goal of the therapist, then, is to help patients with MPD to gather up their scattered selves and assemble them into a functioning whole, a process known as integration.

It is not an easy task. There exists no surefire technique or magic pill, and the speed of recovery depends entirely upon the patient. Many therapists, falling into a common trap, start to imagine each patient as a group of separate people instead of a single, divided person.

Another problem is that not all multiples, as people with MPD are sometimes called, want a unified personality. Some fear the painful process of dredging up long-suppressed memories, a key to recovery. Others worry about the loss of creativity, sometimes even mourning the "death" of their various personalities.

Resistance can be overcome, at least in part, by supplemental techniques such as dance therapy. Therapists often use hypnosis to suggest certain images—an embrace, for example—that symbolically join the disparate selves. And one of the most effective treatments, as illustrated at left, involves expression through art. Many personalities find it easier to release trapped secrets by drawing than by discussing their emotions directly. But even when a patient becomes whole, there is a risk that the personality will splinter again, revealing perhaps another layer of selves.

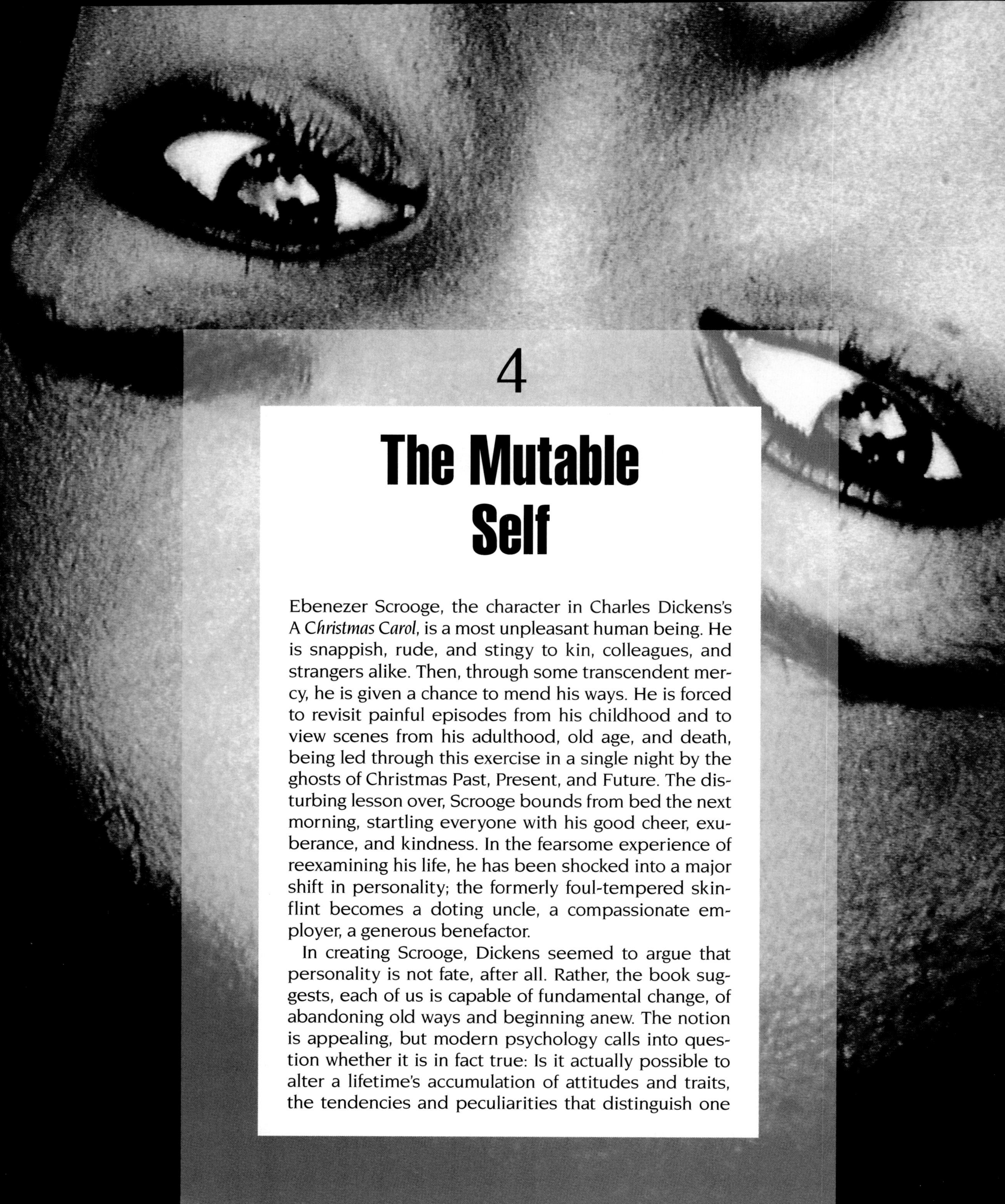

4

The Mutable Self

Ebenezer Scrooge, the character in Charles Dickens's *A Christmas Carol*, is a most unpleasant human being. He is snappish, rude, and stingy to kin, colleagues, and strangers alike. Then, through some transcendent mercy, he is given a chance to mend his ways. He is forced to revisit painful episodes from his childhood and to view scenes from his adulthood, old age, and death, being led through this exercise in a single night by the ghosts of Christmas Past, Present, and Future. The disturbing lesson over, Scrooge bounds from bed the next morning, startling everyone with his good cheer, exuberance, and kindness. In the fearsome experience of reexamining his life, he has been shocked into a major shift in personality; the formerly foul-tempered skinflint becomes a doting uncle, a compassionate employer, a generous benefactor.

In creating Scrooge, Dickens seemed to argue that personality is not fate, after all. Rather, the book suggests, each of us is capable of fundamental change, of abandoning old ways and beginning anew. The notion is appealing, but modern psychology calls into question whether it is in fact true: Is it actually possible to alter a lifetime's accumulation of attitudes and traits, the tendencies and peculiarities that distinguish one

individual from another, and if so, how? Or is it more likely that, on reaching age 30 or thereabouts, we are stuck with who we are, our personalities permanently defined by heredity and experience? The answers to these questions depend in large measure on who is asked—savant or scientist, saint or social worker—and on what criteria are being used to evaluate personality on the one hand, and change on the other.

Whether it is accurate or not, the idea of a changeable psyche is hardly new. Most of the world's great religions not only assert the possibility of change, but offer instances of it. Christianity, for example, is replete with case histories of radical shifts in character. One of the more remarkable is that of Saint Paul.

Paul was once Saul, an agent of the Jewish high priest in charge of arresting followers of the renegade preacher Jesus of Nazareth. Then, as Saul was traveling one day from Jerusalem to Damascus, he was felled by a brilliant light. Blind for three days afterward, he claimed to have conversed with a voice from on high that identified itself as Jesus. When Saul regained his sight, he became the apostle Paul, preeminent publicist for the infant religion of Christianity.

But saints are extraordinary by definition. Is the average person, not touched by the Divine, equally capable of tranforming into a substantially different person?

A random scan of newspapers, magazines, self-help books, and television talk shows would suggest that the answer is yes. People who have undergone major life events, from falling in love to the death of a parent or spouse, frequently seem to experience significant personality changes. Presented with radically altered circumstances, a glimpse of their own mortality, or insights into their characters, they appear to undergo permanent realignment, sometimes exhibiting complete turnarounds in their attitudes and behavior.

Yet there are perhaps just as many stories attesting to the essential immutability of personality: Lottery winners keep the menial jobs they had before getting rich; criminals resist all of society's efforts to rehabilitate them. And everyone knows ordinary people who seem set in their ways, who plod steadily on with the same habits and opinions and routines, no matter what life throws at them.

If everyday experience offers no absolute consensus on whether or not personality is changeable, neither does psychology. Since the founding days of the discipline at the turn of the 20th century, psychologists have debated the question, and still there is no sign of unanimity on the subject. The various sides of the issue fall roughly into two camps.

Trait psychologists argue that the psyche remains stable during adulthood, although behavior may vary according to circumstances. For example, a mother who spends most of her time at home during her twenties, but ranges farther afield in her fifties, may appear to have become less reclusive and more sociable with age. A trait psychologist would hold, however, that she has not really changed at all. When she was a young mother, her children satisfied her gregarious urges; only after the children left home was she prompted to turn elsewhere for company. The woman's degree of sociability remained constant, but her outlets for the characteristic changed with time.

Developmental psychologists, immersed in the study of how personality evolves from birth, have found no evidence that the process ceases a decade or so after puberty. Rather, they hold that people's psyches unfold continually as they mature, noting that individuals hold different views of themselves during childhood, adolescence, early adulthood, middle age, and old age—in effect updating their internal snapshots of themselves as they travel through life.

Guardians of the Soul, Transformers of the Self

Stories of religious conversion and of being "born again" into faith are as common in modern times as they were in centuries past. In psychological terms, the experience almost always involves a wholesale recasting of personality. Individuals typically report that their spiritual awakening leads to more loving, understanding attitudes and relationships with others, as well as to a penetrating reassessment of values, morals, and goals.

For surprising numbers of people today, spiritual transformation finds expression in a belief in a guardian angel. Some tell of a physical presence, often in human form, and of visitations that work dramatic changes in their lives. Others describe a more ethereal phenomenon—ever at hand but often unnoticed. Indeed, some viewers of *Angel of the Blue Dawn* (*left*), painted by Karyn Martin-Kuri in what she calls a state of heightened consciousness, say that it made them aware of their own protector for the very first time.

Although skepticism abounds, of course, there is little denying the profound effect on those who believe in the existence of such beings. As one commentator has put it, for many people angels represent "the triumph of hope over proof."

The impetus for the revisions, which developmentalists consider to be genuine shifts in personality, can come from a number of sources. Some researchers concentrate on stressors—the major events or shocks that life presents from time to time—as precipitating causes of personality change. Stressors may be positive, such as a promotion at work, or negative, such as a death in the family. Other developmental researchers focus more on the conscious efforts people make to transform personality. Vehicles for this sort of volitional change range widely, from 12-step programs such as Alcoholics Anonymous to the discipline of martial arts and the systematic courting of risk.

Each one of these avenues to self-exploration and self-improvement would doubtless have confounded Sigmund Freud, the architect of psychoanalysis, who believed that the study of personality—and the manipulation of it—were properly the province of experts. Nevertheless, even Freud would to some degree have shared the self-helpers' belief in the mutability of personality.

Freud's most significant contributions to psychology lay in his theories about the forces that mold personality in infancy and childhood, rather than in any notions of how the psyche changes over the course of a lifetime. Thus, although he taught that people suffering psychological disorders of one sort or another can respond to the ministrations of his psychoanalytic method, he did not see the evolution of the self as a goal to be pursued.

Carl Jung disagreed with his mentor Freud on this issue as he did on many others. Not only did Jung theorize that personality adjusts fluidly to circumstance, he also believed in the possibility of a process called individuation, in which people work intentionally toward making their own personalities stand out from the collective mass of attitudes and behaviors. To do so is no small undertaking. Not everyone makes the attempt, and only dedicated individuals succeed.

Developmental psychologist Erik Erikson, who refined Freud's work in many respects, agreed with Jung's view of human possibility but saw the process as rather more common and accessible to anyone than did Jung. Erikson proposed that personality evolves through the synthesis of opposing pulls on the psyche—the need to be alone versus the need for intimacy, for example. He accepted as a foregone conclusion a lifelong course of personality development, in which adults pass through three stages: In their twenties and thirties, they learn to forge intimate relationships; in their forties and fifties they focus on creativity, including guiding and encouraging younger people; and after age 65, they work at resolving internal conflicts to arrive at what Erikson called integrity.

A great many psychologists today hold with Erikson that personality is a variable, not a constant. Developmentalists may continue to dicker over precisely what changes and how, but they accept that the adult psyche goes on changing with age just as the adult body does.

By the 1950s, psychologists could map with confidence the critical formative periods of childhood and adolescence, when behavior may undergo striking shifts, seemingly overnight; in most healthy people, the shifts culminate in a stable adult personality. Few researchers, however, went on to till the ground broken by Erikson in his formulation of the developmental stages of adulthood. This void was addressed during the 1970s in the work of psychology professor Daniel Levinson of Yale and psychiatrist Roger Gould of the University of California at Los Angeles.

Levinson viewed his work as a link extending the intellectual chain joining Freud, Jung, and Erikson. In his studies, which were done exclusively with men, Levinson observed that personality development proceeded through alternate stages of stability and instability, forming a pattern of crisis and resolution that allowed a man's life to be conceived of as segments. With views shaped—and limited—by the gender of his subjects, he theorized that men march through a set of clearly demarcated stages as they age, for the most part independent of any particular events that occur in their lives.

After leaving home, usually between ages 22 and 28, a man begins making his own way, without benefit of much experience and therefore rather clumsily at first. It is during this stage that he mates and fathers children. From 28 to 33, said Levinson, a man reevaluates the choices he has made and either affirms or rejects them. He may divorce a first wife, for example, or quit a long-held job. From 33 to 40, a man advances in his career, first gaining a mentor, then advancing beyond that relationship to become "his own man." But at 40 he hits a rough patch and must deal with problems that he has ignored or been unaware of. Confused, he falls prey to a kind of emotional paralysis, struggling to come to terms with his professional failures, perhaps, or signs of decline in his aging body. He entertains doubts about his sexuality, or he questions his commitment to his work and his family. After this period of turmoil, a man reaches at around 45 an ability to view himself with greater satisfaction and give more freely of himself to others.

In contrast to Levinson, Roger Gould studied the lives of women as well as men, but he came to substantially the same conclusion, that the lives of human beings divide into distinct stages. He said that usually between about ages 28 and 34, once people settle somewhat into workaday life of home and office, they take stock of their lives and struggle to reconcile reality with the ideal of their desires: Am I in the right job? Am I with the right mate? Between 35 and 45, a person grapples with the profound issues of evil, violence, and death—a moral and spiritual exercise whose implications, more abstract when the individual was younger, can now be dauntingly concrete: Should she institutionalize a senile parent? Will he cheat on his income tax? Around age 50 individuals who have successfully navigated the shoals of becoming an adult achieve a resolution of the conflicts bred in childhood, along with a sense of being more in control of their destiny.

Under normal circumstances, Levinson and Gould would have shared their work with a small cadre in their field, publishing in the appropriate journals and then standing back while their peers scrutinized the details. But this time, as happens occasionally, a journalist seized upon the research results and conveyed them to a far wider public. Author Gail Sheehy, in preparing to write about the nature of adulthood, interviewed the two personality investigators at length and incorporated the information she gleaned into a manuscript. The resulting book, called *Passages*, was an instant bestseller.

Published in 1976, *Passages* made the world privy to the conclusions Levinson and Gould had drawn from observing the influences of aging on personality. Of all the things that Levinson told Sheehy about the stages of development in male personality, the potentially calamitous period beginning at age 40 seemed to strike a special chord with the public. Sheehy called it the midlife passage. More commonly known as the midlife crisis, this personality shakeup can be so disturbing, Sheehy wrote, that people may resort to sexual dalliances, physical risk taking, or other lifestyle changes in a quest to rediscover what has been missing from their lives. This is the time when the number of divorces soars, as do job switches, admissions to psychiatric wards, and suicides. Later, Sheehy, along with psychologists and feminist thinkers, would propose that women undergo a similar crisis, in the form of empty nest syndrome, after their last child has left home, and of menopause, a physiological retooling that can also affect the psyche.

In large measure, Levinson and Gould were theorizers rather than experimenters. Having studied no more than a few score individuals, they produced grand generalizations about humanity but made little effort to gather supporting statistical evidence. Their colleagues pointed out that the patterns Levinson and Gould had outlined were unlikely to prove universal. Their subjects were, by and large, well-educated, well-to-do, middle-class Americans—hardly a suitable yardstick for speculation about all of humanity. Critics also doubted that every person would progress through life's supposed segments at the same pace. At best, age-related stages could be construed only as a sketchy aid to understanding, not as a hard-and-fast schedule.

Determined to settle this matter, a few trait psychologists set about looking for solid evidence of adult personality development—not certain that they would find any. Notable among these researchers were Robert R. McCrae and Paul T. Costa Jr., both based at the Gerontology Research Center of the National Institutes of Health in Baltimore, Maryland. Beginning as early as 1965, these future advocates of the Five Factor Model

Reshaping Personality with Therapeutic Drugs

Much to their surprise, psychiatrists sometimes find that a medication prescribed for mental illness has gone beyond treating the condition to revamping the patient's personality. One such drug is Prozac, an antidepressant that is also effective against obsessive-compulsive disorder (*page* 75). A substantial minority of all Prozac patients report a change far greater than the standard mood-leveling brought about by other antidepressants. They become, in the words of one man who took it, "better than well," as though the drug had eliminated character traits that had prevented these patients from realizing their full potential. In a typical case, one woman gained assertiveness and lost the self-doubt she had harbored all her life. As a result, she was able to excel at a demanding job and take charge of her previously disappointing personal life.

Scientists are well aware of the physiological effects of Prozac: It blocks the reabsorption of the neurotransmitter serotonin by neurons after a neural impulse crosses a synapse. But the reasons for Prozac's special efficacy at altering personality remain a mystery.

Researchers also marvel at Clozapine, which is frequently used to treat schizophrenia. Like Prozac it works by affecting neurotransmitter levels, in this case the relative amounts of serotonin and dopamine at each synapse. But rather than transforming personality, it seems to restore personality traits that had been masked by the mental illness.

Although more than half of the schizophrenics who take Clozapine experience some relief, a full 20 percent stage a recovery so profound that doctors refer to it as an "awakening." The voices and delusions that have besieged them for years vanish, and with the help of therapists they can start the long process of becoming the people they once were. In the words of one recovering schizophrenic who had attempted suicide, Clozapine took her from "hating the sunshine in the mornings to loving it."

Brandon Fitch, a 19-year-old who owes his recovery from schizophrenia to Clozapine, cuts loose with a dance teacher at a prom thrown for Clozapine patients at Cleveland's Case Western Reserve University in 1992. The event was intended to make up for celebrations missed by victims once lost in the disease's grip.

The Role of Therapy

Psychiatrists emphasize that although drugs such as Prozac and Clozapine can greatly benefit the mentally ill, conventional psychotherapy is still a vital part of any treatment. Most view drugs as "cotherapists" that aid, but do not replace, so-called talk therapy.

A 1992 experiment performed at UCLA supports this view. Researchers treated one group of patients suffering from obsessive-compulsive disorder with Prozac and another solely with behavioral therapy. A comparison of before-and-after PET scans, at right, shows that both groups had similar diminished activity in a part of the brain (*indicated by white arrows*) believed to play a role in the disorder.

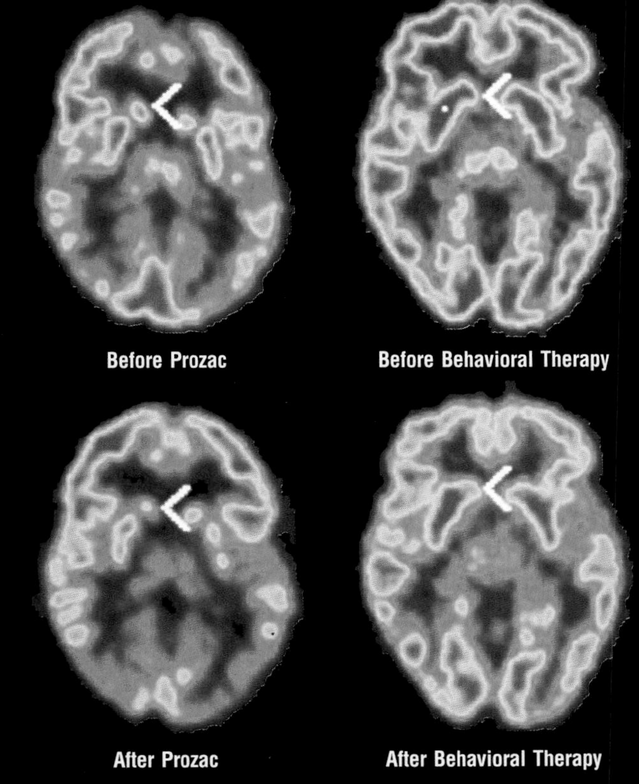

Before Prozac

Before Behavioral Therapy

After Prozac

After Behavioral Therapy

After winning $40 million in the Illinois state lottery in 1984, Michael Wittkowski credited friends and family with helping save him from "getting haughty." Wittkowski—shown here with his wife in front of one of their investments, a liquor store selling lottery tickets—is among those lottery winners who insist that instant wealth had little effect on their core values.

(*pages* 32-33), which distills more than half a century's work in the field of trait psychology, sifted through masses of data and conducted tests on adults from all walks of life.

Working tirelessly to gauge the mutability of underlying personality traits, McCrae and Costa evaluated the methods of developmental psychologists, assimilated the results of hundreds of age-related psychological studies, and carried out their own tests. They and others found almost nothing to support the hypotheses of developmentalists such as Levinson and Gould. In particular, virtually no data bore out the existence of the midlife crisis of men in their early forties. The crisis was a phantom. Similarly, McCrae and Costa found that divorce numbers peaked for people in their twenties, while suicide took its greatest toll among teens and the elderly. Furthermore, psychiatric admissions did not reach their highest level among 40-year-olds, but among people in their late twenties.

As a result of their efforts, Costa and McCrae concluded that personality is not, in fact, changeable. Rather, it is characterized by stability. The two scientists presented their findings for general audiences in the 1990 book *Personality in Adulthood*, which relentlessly attacked the developmentalist camp. According to the two trait psychologists, people demonstrate impressive constancy over the course of adulthood, exhibiting much the same personality at 80 as at 28. "When children leave home, when aged parents require care, when one retires from a lifelong occupation, there are profound changes in the daily routines that constitute the bulk of behavior," the two researchers said, "but these changes do not amount to changes in personality, and they come about in response to external necessity rather than internal development."

Psychologists have identified three chief reasons that personality tends to be stable. First, people's views of themselves, as measured by self-assessment tests, vary little during adulthood. Second, people tend toward associations that reinforce their personalities. Extraverts seek out occupations and spouses, for example, compatible with their inclinations; doing so tends to reinforce them. Third, much research indicates that certain traits such as neuroticism and openness have a large genetic component and thus would not be expected to change significantly over time.

But if personality is unchanging, how had the developmental camp gone so far astray? In the main, McCrae and Costa said, those researchers had confused external circumstances with internal makeup, mistaking people's life structure for their personality. The shape of one's life, they argued, depends less on inherent traits than on accidents of birth, health, and wealth. A person, whatever his or her core nature, functions amid a web of influences, bound by familial and social ties, subject to conditions and obligations not fully under his or her control. So the trajectory of a life cannot be read as identical to the trajectory of personality. "Life does not lead to change or growth in personality," McCrae and Costa wrote, "but it allows a fascinating variety of situations in which personal dispositions, for good or ill, play a part."

Some people, for instance, switch careers several times during adulthood, attaining one goal only to pursue another. For McCrae and Costa, these revisions constitute evidence of consistency in personality, not change. In fact, tests of people who continue setting new goals for themselves throughout life almost invariably show that they have a high measure of a basic trait called openness to experience, a factor that drives their search for the next challenge. Many seemingly radical personality shifts may be better explained as energies refocused. The biblical character Saul, for example, had been as zealous an enforcer of the will of the

Jewish ecclesiastical hierarchy as he became a proselytizer under his new identity as the Christian apostle Paul, suggesting that his essential nature remained the same even after his religious conversion. Only the object of his allegiance changed.

If the stability suggested by McCrae and Costa dimmed the hopes of believers in perfectibility, there was also good news. "If we don't grow, neither do we decline," the scientists noted. We are not doomed to conform to the nasty social stereotypes of old age, to become more cranky, dotty, and rigid. While most people lose a degree of short-term memory with age and become a bit slower to grasp unfamiliar information (due in all likelihood to the loss of connections between brain cells), they are not destined to become, say, mired in nostalgia or unbearably closed-minded—unless dreaminess or rigidity was part of their makeup in youth.

Evidence supporting the trait psychologists' view of a fixed adult personality comes not only from the laboratory, but also from accounts of ordinary people confronting extraordinary circumstances—lottery winners, for example. Winning the lottery is a classic stressor, the kind of event that developmentalists would expect to cause a dramatic change in personality. Indeed, for some winners, taking home the big prize can turn out to be a most unpleasant experience, as they are bombarded by requests for donations, targeted by con men, and badgered by grasping relatives, neighbors, and friends. Yet the stress rarely, if ever, results in a permanent personality change. Sharon Barnes, for one, took home $16 million in a 1988 Ohio lottery. Instead of splurging with her winnings, this thrifty midwestern loan officer started taking sewing lessons. "I'm still me," said Barnes. "I was brought up that way."

As a matter of fact, psychologist Avshalom Caspi and his colleagues at the University of Wisconsin have found that people's character traits are more likely to intensify than to change under stress. Caspi carried out a retrospective analysis of men who experienced the Great Depression of the 1930s, for example, and found that those who were irritable or aggressive beforehand generally became more so during those precarious times. He also found similar evidence of what he calls accentuation in other measures of personality. Shy people, for example, tend to become even more bashful during life's major—and thus stressful—transitions: from single to married, from childlessness to parenthood, and from college into the world of work and a career.

Many observers agree that trait psychologists have shown all but conclusively that personality does not evolve according to an innate choreography, as developmentalists had proposed. Nevertheless, personality is not immutable for everyone under all circumstances—if only because in matters of the mind there always seem to be exceptions to the general rule. Unusual as they may be, a substantial number of cases have been documented in which personality undergoes significant change in response to harsh stresses of great intensity, long duration, or both.

War is the classic example. During World War I, physicians began noticing major personality upheavals in soldiers returning from the trenches—alterations that were lumped under the general term *shell shock*. Again during World War II, military hospitals became filled with servicemen whose personality traits had changed drastically under the horrors of combat. In the 1970s, psychologists began cataloging the dozens of personality anomalies they were finding in troops returning from the Vietnam War—irregularities that might persist for months or years. The doctors dubbed this spectrum of symptoms the posttraumatic stress syndrome.

Generally, the disorder involves people reliving some part of their disturbing experiences, either in dreams or in waking fantasies. The victims become jumpy, irritable, and anxious, even paranoid. They are often unable to maintain personal relationships or to hold down jobs, and they may slide into alcohol or drug abuse, exacerbating their mental instability. The sufferers may reject help from loved ones—and be rejected in return. And as their illness progresses, they may develop chronic emotional debilities, including severe depression and attacks of panic or rage.

Combatants are not the only ones to suffer from posttraumatic stress syndrome. Among civilian survivors of Nazi concentration camps, for instance, and the nuclear bombings of Hiroshima and Nagasaki during World War II, many confirm the remarkable resiliency of the human spirit. Others, however, reveal the damage that severe stress can wreak on the personality. Regardless of how well adjusted these individuals had been before, some of those who lived through such horrors have spent much of the rest of their lives tortured by fear. One former death-camp inmate reported that years after he was freed, he still panicked at the sound of a siren or the sight of someone in uniform. Reported another survivor: "Nights most often are so terrible that I scream and have to be awakened by my husband."

Decades after the atomic blast at Hiroshima, some Japanese who had been in the city remained tormented by vivid memories of victims, doomed by radiation poisoning, wandering amid the rubble with their skin sloughing off. Psychiatrist and historian Robert Jay Lifton, who began studying Hiroshima survivors while working at Yale University, identified four typical psychological phases, beginning with a numbness so profound that it virtually negated personality. As radiation poisoning spread, the numbness was followed by fear, then by obsession with the genetic effects of radiation on future offspring, and finally by a lifelong guilt for having lived when others had died.

Such survivors share in common what must surely be the most powerful negative stressor: proximity to death. In recent years, however, psychologists have been able to study an entirely new class of survivors—those who have, however briefly, not only experienced the closeness of death, but in a sense also tasted the reality. These veterans of the near-death experience, or NDE, have grown more numerous as advances in emergency medicine allow doctors to revive patients who not so many years ago would have been declared dead.

People who survive a brush with death typically report it as a rapturous event. "Before you is this most magnificent, just gorgeous blue-white light," reported a man who had nearly been crushed to death when a truck he was repairing fell onto his chest. "It is brighter than a light that would

British truckdriver Howard Ainsley-Knowles, pictured with his wife, suffers the emotional torment of posttraumatic stress syndrome. He developed the condition after another driver, bent on suicide, crashed headlong into his rig at more than 100 miles per hour. The trucker's symptoms, which include adrenaline surges, flashbacks, nightmares, and guilt, are typically associated with veterans of brutal warfare, but mental-health professionals now often diagnose the disorder in survivors of natural catastrophes, child and sexual abuse, serious accidents, and kidnapping. Diarist Samuel Pepys observed the telltale signs of the then-unnamed malady in London residents after the great fire of 1666.

immediately blind you, but this absolutely does not hurt your eyes at all." An intense light of some kind is a feature common to many near-death experiences, as is a sensation of being in the presence of great power and knowledge. "You realize," this man continued, "that you are suddenly in communication with absolute, total knowledge. You can think of a question and immediately know the answer to it. As simple as that."

Often accompanying these sensations is one of utter satisfaction and perfection. "If you took the 1,000 best things that ever happened to you in your life," said another survivor, "and multiplied by a million, maybe you could get close to this feeling," which also contains a strong element of sanctuary and tranquillity. "I was an infinite being in perfection," this woman recounted. "And love and safety and security and knowing that nothing could happen to you."

About one-third of all near-death experiences feature a so-called life review. One woman who was nearly killed in a car wreck watched her life go by "click, click in a split second. It was all black and white and I saw everything. I saw my life pass right by me." Said another survivor: "You are shown your life—and you do the judging. Are you able to forgive yourself for not doing the things you should have done and some little cheaty things that maybe you've done in life? This is the judgment."

Such experiences very often seem to bring about a personality change in their wake. Many survivors declare that they no longer fear death—or much of anything else, for that matter. Day-to-day worries become of minimal concern to them, old ambitions seem irrelevant, and peace settles like a blanket over their psyches.

In 1983 Bruce Greyson, then a psychiatrist at the University of Michigan Hospital in Ann Arbor, did personality surveys of 264 people, 89 of them survivors of a near-death experience, and found that the survivors professed to care far less about material and social success than did the other people in the study, who closely resembled them in education and professional status. Greyson speculated that a near-death experience "may leave the individual with a primary sense of worth and meaning not contingent upon conventional measures of success." Consequently, Greyson concluded, such people may become less anxious or disturbed in other ways about their relative success or failure in life, regarding themselves from a transcendental perspective.

University of Connecticut psychologist Kenneth Ring began studying near-death experiences in the late 1970s. Like Greyson, Ring also found what he construed to be personality shifts associated with the phenomenon. Ring, whose data included the results from questionnaires filled out by hundreds of subjects, found that the changes ranged from mild to extensive—from a mere boost of self-confidence or self-worth to a new passion for life. "I have a fierce desire to live every wonderful moment of as many days as I can manage to be gifted with," one survivor said. To read other accounts is to hear repeated echoes of wholesale reformation: "I have changed from a very shy, introverted person to an extravert. All the way out!" reported another subject. "I now talk in public. I could never have made a speech in my life before."

Ring suggests that these changes sometimes come about by means of a kind of accelerated psychoanalysis. When some people replay their entire emotional history during the near-death experience, they gain insights that in psychotherapy often lead to a resolution of conflicts and an improved mental state. However, Ring also speculates that a different mechanism may be at work, one that is akin to certain religions of antiquity in which a select few were initiated into a cult through rites aimed at transforming consciousness. In that sense, the psychologist says, NDEs represent "a modern version, cloaked in the symbols of our own time, of the ancient mystery teachings concerning life, death, and regeneration."

The evidence assembled so far by psychologists suggests that personality is changed, if at all, only by chance encounters with life's most powerful stressors. Yet untold numbers of people spend hour after hour in various forms of therapy, hoping to reduce anxiety, say, or to make themselves less reclusive, or to otherwise change elements of their personalities that they regard as unsatisfactory.

The chances of remaking personality, say trait psychologists, are small. Talking with a psychiatrist will not change an introvert into an extravert or a pessimist into an optimist. At best, a great investment of therapeutic energy can be expected to yield only incremental benefits.

But human beings are nothing if not creatures of hope. Those who enter formal therapy (*pages* 121-131) are but a small percentage of the many more who seek ways of becoming happier, better adjusted, and more fulfilled through improved self-knowledge. Although the methods are sometimes denigrated by the psychology establishment, millions of people engage in self-analysis or join group forums to discuss their addictions or other ailments and conditions. Still others take part in inspirational mass meetings designed to help participants learn new ways of being.

Any such effort to change personality requires a clear-eyed view of what personality is. One useful perspective comes from the concept of personae in psychology. Derived from the Latin word for the masks that Roman actors used as emblems for the characters they played, personae are different aspects of personality that emerge according to the circumstances. At work, for example, any of us may show elements of personality different from those that appear at home. One mask may serve for peers, another for superiors, with others perhaps on call for dealing with men or with women. For someone who is unaware of these masks—which tend to come forward automatically and unbidden—simply identifying them, exploring them, and understanding their effects on others can be of great benefit. The very act of gaining some measure of control over one's personae may thus produce changes in personality that can appear to be deep and far reaching.

One route to this kind of awareness is the Myers-Briggs Type Indicator, or MBTI. Introduced in the 1950s—and subsequently imitated in widely available personality surveys—Myers-Briggs springs from the adage "Know thyself." Before one can alter the self, in other words, one must first appraise the self in its totality.

To this end, an American woman, Isabel Myers, set about to develop what has become one of the most effective tools available for performing this subtle task. Myers's work was inspired by her mother, Katharine Briggs, an avid reader who—though untutored in psychology—embraced Carl Jung's work in categorizing the characteristics that constitute personality. In the 1940s, Myers taught herself statistics and principles of psychology testing with the intention of turning typology toward the practical end of smoothing relations between people. The result was a disarmingly simple questionnaire designed to classify people by Jungian types. Lacking formal credentials, Myers spent years in a determined effort to win acceptance from the psychology establishment, and with time, the MBTI has gained respectability and come into widespread use.

The test is based on Jung's sets of opposing human characteristics: extraversion (E) versus introversion (I);

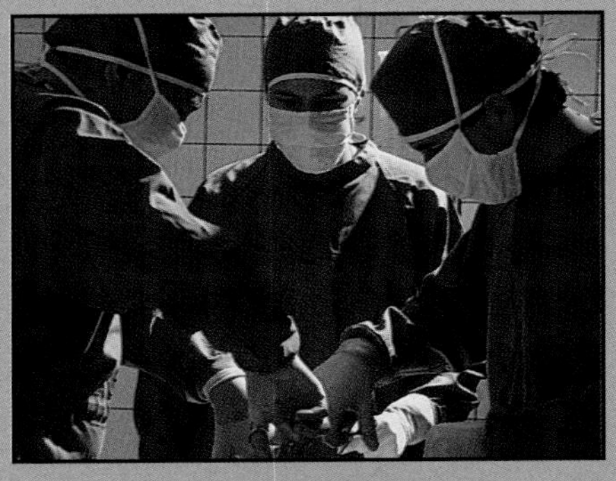

sensation (S) versus intuition (N), which addresses a preference for concreteness or abstraction; thinking (T) versus feeling (F), a scale marked by people who rely on logic at one end and emotional responses at the other; and judgment (J) versus perception (P), which differentiates between those who constantly evaluate events against an internal standard and others who are more likely to accept things as they are.

More than 100 neutrally phrased questions about preferred or habitual ways of thinking and acting appear on the test. From two responses to each question, people taking the MBTI must choose the one that better describes their own tendencies. Honest answers, if not assured, are encouraged by the fact that neither answer is right or wrong. Perhaps more significant, someone unfamiliar with the MBTI cannot easily tell which characteristic each question addresses. Any attempt to cheat could thus have unpredictable consequences.

Of 16 possible profiles, the test results will suggest which one a person fits (*pages* 30-31). When Myers took the test, for example, her answers identified her as an INFP. Her mother, on the other hand, emerged as an INFJ. That is, both mother and daughter tended to be introverts (I), were more intuitive (N) than sensing when reaching conclusions, and acted in response to their feelings more than to logic. They differed, however, in the last of the four scales, where Briggs tended to be more decisive than her daughter.

The Myers-Briggs Type Indicator can be administered only by a psychologist or career counselor, although look-alike versions of it are available for self-testing. While the MBTI is perhaps best known as an aid in career planning (*page* 115), that was not, for Myers, its main purpose. She believed that the point of classifying personality was to expand human potential, to enable individuals to find, as she put it, "a rationale for many of the personality differences they encounter in their work or must deal with in their private lives."

At the root of strife between people, Myers believed, lies an incomprehension of individuality and of different styles, a lack of understanding that could be monumentally damaging when played out in a national or international arena. The better each of us understands our own psychological type, Myers believed, the more insight we gain into other people's outlooks and the better we can ease tensions, whether by being more accepting of other people or by adapt-

ISTJ
Pollution Control
Police Officers
Steelworkers
Managers
Corrections Sergeants
Public Accountants
School Bus Drivers
Bank Employees
School Principals
Managers: Executive

ISFJ
Clergy and Religious
Nurses: All Types
Clerical Supervisors
Teachers: Grades 1 to 12
Doctors of Osteopathy
School Bus Drivers
Teachers: Preschool
Social Services Admin.
Teachers: Speech Therapy
Teacher Aides

INFJ
Clergy and Religious
Fine Artists
Consultants: Education
Physicians: Pathology
Teachers
Social Workers
Architects
Media Specialists
Physicians: Psychiatry
Doctors of Osteopathy

INTJ
Architects
Computer Professionals
Consultants: Management
Lawyers
Managers: Executive
Human Resource Planners
Research Workers
Social Services Workers
Engineers
Scientists: Life and Physical

ISTP
Police Officers
Farmers
Air Force Personnel
Engineers: Electronic
Technicians: Electronic
Coal Miners
Steelworkers
Transportation Operatives
Dental Hygienists
Service Workers

ISFP
Storekeepers and Clerks
Surveyors
Clerical Supervisors
Dental Assistants
Radiology Technicians
Bookkeepers
Operatives: All Types
Cleaning Services
Carpenters
Nurses

INFP
Fine Artists
Physicians: Psychiatry
Psychologists
Architects
Editors and Reporters
Research Assistants
Entertainers
Journalists
Counselors: General
Religious Educators

INTP
Entertainers
Computer Professionals
Architects
Research Assistants
Fine Artists
Computer Programmers
Lawyers
Managers: Executive
Scientists
Pharmacists

ESTP
Marketing Personnel
Radiology Technicians
Police Officers
Service Workers
Carpenters
Sales Clerks
Managers: Small Business
Auditors
Craft Workers
Farmers

ESFP
Childcare Workers
Receptionists/Typists
Transportation Operatives
Respiratory Therapists
Factory Supervisors
Library Attendants
Cashiers
Designers
Clerical Supervisors
Recreation Attendants

ENFP
Social Workers
Counselors
Journalists
Teachers: Arts and Music
Research Assistants
Entertainers
Psychologists
Clergy and Religious
Radiology Technicians
Musicians and Composers

ENTP
Photographers
Marketing Personnel
Sales Agents
Journalists
Actors
Computer Analysts
Credit Investigators
Physicians: Psychiatry
Engineers
Construction Laborers

ESTJ
Managers: Executive
Managers: Fire
Managers: Police Officers
Purchasing Agents
Teachers: Trade
School Principals
Managers: Financial
Bank Employees
Factory Supervisors
Community Health

ESFJ
Clergy and Religious
Secretaries: Medical
Hairdressers
Teachers: Grades 1 to 12
Receptionists
Restaurant Workers
Student Personnel Admin.
Home Economists
Dental Assistants
Bank Employees

ENFJ
Clergy and Religious
Home Economists
Teachers
Actors
Entertainers
Consultants: General
Optometrists
Counselors: General
Musicians and Composers
Pharmacists

ENTJ
Consultants: Management
Lawyers
Human Resource Planners
Managers/Administrators
Managers: Executive
Credit Investigators
Marketing Personnel
Computer Specialists
Labor Relations Workers
Psychologists

Career and Character: Finding a Match

To a greater extent than might be imagined, what we choose to do for a living reflects the kind of people we are. The originators of the Myers-Briggs Type Indicator (*pages* 30-31) first quantified this relationship in the 1970s by surveying the most common occupations for each of the 16 personality types they had identified. In subsequent years, responses tabulated from more than 250,000 people led to the creation of the table above, which lists the 10 careers chosen most frequently by the members of each type.

The results offer an interesting perspective on what can be described as the personality of certain occupations. Musicians and composers, for instance, tend to be either ENFPs or ENFJs: extraverted, intuitive, feeling, and either perceiving or judging. Some professions attract people from several related types, as is the case with computer jobs: Although they fall into four different categories, people in these fields share the attributes of being intuitive (rather than sensing) and thinking (rather than feeling).

Career counselors often use studies such as this to help guide their clients in choosing a first job or changing directions. Such information can also play a role in therapy, providing new hope for people wrestling with dissatisfaction about themselves: Rather than trying to change some fundamental aspect of their personality, the solution may lie in finding a career that matches better who they are.

ing our own personae to accommodate those whose personalities tend to clash with our own.

Because the MBTI assumes a healthy personality, the test has little value for those who suffer from pronounced neuroses or from identifiable personality disorders and their consequences, which in some cases include drug and alcohol abuse. For such people, insights to their behavior commonly require much more time and dedication and may come only at great emotional cost.

Perhaps the single most widely practiced method for dealing with these often severe personality problems emerged not from academia or clinical psychology but from the experience of former New York City stockbroker Bill Wilson, a reformed alcoholic and inventor of the life-changing 12-step program embodied in Alcoholics Anonymous (AA).

As a down-and-out drunk who had tried and failed at every tactic medicine had to offer for kicking his habit, a despairing Wilson encountered in the 1930s a member of a British evangelical organization known as the Oxford Group. Spiritual enlightenment followed. For Wilson, the experience amounted to a change in the deepest realms of his personality. Before, he had been destructively self-centered. In the wake of his transformation, he turned outward and began building "a society of alcoholics, each identifying with and transmitting his experience to the next."

Over time, Wilson formulated the 12 rules, or steps, upon which Alcoholics Anonymous rests. By the early 1990s, nearly 90,000 AA groups had sprung up worldwide, and an estimated two million people were following—or trying to follow—its precepts. Taking Step 1 ("We admitted we were powerless over alcohol—that our lives had become unmanageable") led in time to taking Steps 4 and 5 ("Made a searching and fearless moral inventory of ourselves" and "Admitted to God, to ourselves, and to another human being the exact nature of our wrongs") and eventually to an endpoint ("Having had a spiritual awakening as a result of these steps, we tried to carry this message to others and to practice these principles in all our affairs").

In conceiving his program, Wilson put forward a spiritual message but promoted no single religious viewpoint. AA, as it continues today, propounds a moral realism in which people gain self-acceptance, clarity, confidence, and faith, bolstered by long-term group and individual support. In explaining the apparent success of his method in a letter to Carl Jung, Wilson once wrote that "most conversion experiences, whatever their variety, do have a common denominator of ego collapse at depth." Faced with this obliteration of his personality, the alcoholic must realize that medical science alone cannot cure him, and that he must turn to a higher power for help.

During the 1980s, a host of other 12-step programs appeared, riding on the success of AA, which by then had helped hundreds of thousands of people climb aboard, and stay on, the wagon. A partial list of the AA follow-ons includes Alateen and Al-Atot (for children of alcoholics), Cocaine Anonymous, Bulimics/Anorexics Anonymous, Gamblers Anonymous, Fundamentalists Anonymous, Overeaters Anonymous, Shoplifters Anonymous, and Workaholics Anonymous. All have put Wilson's trademark dozen steps at the center of their approach and stage weekly meetings where members share life histories with one another and often select other members as sponsors who offer encouragement and help forestall backsliding.

All of these quests for personal revision—for overcoming the failures, limitations, uncertainties, pain, and losses experienced throughout life—can lead beyond the realm of the mind into that of the body. Scientists have confirmed, for example, that a bright

Mind Control and Its Controversial "Cure"

Religious and political cults are often accused of gaining new members through so-called mind control—manipulative psychological techniques that use forms of hypnosis and high-pressure group dynamics. Distraught family members and friends, intent on rescuing their loved ones, sometimes resort to a controversial approach known as deprogramming—a tactic that critics contend is just as coercive.

Deprogramming was first developed in the 1970s by Ted Patrick, a former aide to California governor Ronald Reagan. Patrick's technique involves coaxing presumed victims away from their group or actually abducting them. Either way, the victims then spend several days in a locked room while Patrick reasons with, browbeats, and sometimes even physically intimidates them into renouncing allegiance to the cult. He claims to have conducted some 2,600 successful deprogrammings using these methods, but he has also spent time in prison on kidnapping charges.

Deprogrammers, challenged on both legal grounds and ethical grounds, often respond with a "fight fire with fire" argument. According to them, their extreme measures are entirely justified and are only as ruthless as those used by the cults to warp their victims' minds in the first place.

smile can be the cause—as well as an effect—of a happy feeling. Although the mood elevation may be short-lived, it is real nonetheless and establishes the possibility that other kinds of physical activity might influence temperament.

The notion is inherent in many forms of Asian philosophy. From earliest times, Asian thinkers have drawn no distinction between the corporeal and the spiritual, seeing them as but different forms of a single force that animates the entire cosmos. For many Asians, honing the body is tantamount to reconfiguring the character.

Early on any morning, for example, a visitor strolling through the parks and squares of a Chinese city is bound to see dozens of men and women gyrating slowly through a series of artful poses, kicks, and thrusts. These are the ritual motions of tai chi chuan, an ancient form of exercise that involves two interlocking disciplines: *qigong*, or "breath work"; and *wu shu*, a method of self-defense. Upon mastering both of these aspects, a person is said to be capable of regulating the flow of chi, or qi, the vital energy or essential life force that pervades both mind and body, as it does all the cosmos. A person who can regulate qi attains the Tao—the "Way."

A common element in many Eastern philosophies, the Way is both an endpoint and a process; in Western terms it might be roughly expressed as "going with the flow." But, as tai chi teaches, following the Way is hardly the same as lapsing into passivity. Instead, tai chi promotes an intensely vital form of relaxation, a looseness and openness of body that will be mirrored by an openness of mind. The Chinese take this enhanced confidence matter-of-factly as the natural result of channeling qi, which despite being unmeasurable by Western scientific methods underlies most of traditional Chinese medicine. Students of tai chi say that it induces an "egoless calm," a centeredness that radiates into the rest of their lives.

Psychologists fascinated by the supposed transformational powers of martial arts such as tai chi, the more

In a Shanghai city park, residents seek to harmonize themselves with the world through the slow and deliberate movements of their daily tai chi exercise. Some practitioners claim that the discipline of body and mind produces a calm, "centered" outlook.

aggressive tae kwon do from Korea, and other such disciplines have made numerous studies of practitioners and have found that adepts do seem to be remarkably self-confident and secure in their identities. Because many sports have also been shown to boost players' self-confidence, such changes may well be due to the pride that people take in mastering new skills. But one psychologist, Thomas Nardi of Pace University in New York, has suggested that the cause lies elsewhere—in the martial arts teacher, who performs a role akin to that of a therapist, addressing pupils' psyches as much as their bodies.

If the deliberate elegance of the martial arts is one way to lift personality onto a new plane, certain high-risk sports are deemed by some bold experimenters to be another. Those in search of such jolting change may take their choice from a wide range of activities, from free climbing (scaling rocks solo and without the aid of pitons and ropes) to skydiving. Enthusiasts have claimed that such mentally and physically demanding activities boost self-esteem. Says a woman bungee jumper, for example, "If you can prove to yourself that you can do something that is very scary, you can carry that confidence with you into any situation."

Some experts contend that the long-term personality benefits of high-risk sports are minimal. "The immediate high is enough in itself," according to sports psychologist Bruce Ogilvie, who adds that "risk taking isn't likely to transfer into other areas of life." But other researchers believe that taking risks answers a primordial need, reminding human beings of a time in their collective past when the daily routine involved dodging a mastodon or fording a raging river as opposed to ducking the boss or crawling along a congested freeway to get home. A risk taker, by surviving, transcends workaday drudgery and demonstrates an ability to meet any challenge and to expand horizons, not only at play but also at work.

To journalist Ralph Keyes, who interviewed nearly 1,000 such daredevils for his book *Chancing It: Why We Take Risks*, bungee jumpers and their ilk are seeking the same "natural high" that marathoners and participants in other endurance sports are said to crave. This feeling of euphoria and well-being results from the release of endorphins, the brain's own opiate-like chemicals, in response to physical stress. Keyes believes that bungee jumpers, whitewater kayakers, and other risk takers, having become addicted to their own endorphins, are always on the hunt for the next rush.

If the physiological consequences of daredeviltry can transform the personality, much as some extremes of personality can be controlled through medication, it may well be possible that medication can also transform—making the timid bold or a suspicious person into a more trusting one. Prozac may be just such a transforming drug. Widely available since the late 1980s as a treatment for depression, this addition to the medical arsenal is unlike most antidepressant drugs. Rather than helping people feel like their old selves, Prozac seems to give many people a brand new self. A depressed woman named Tess is just one example from an ever-lengthening catalog of such results in both men and women.

Tess had been raised in near poverty by an alcoholic father and a mother who suffered from depression. Yet in spite of the disadvantages inherent in such an upbringing, Tess became a skilled organizer and morale booster much valued in the business world for her ability to put floundering companies on a track toward success. Although she had a history of unsatisfactory relationships with men, Tess was to all appearances a solid citizen whose personality was well within the normal range.

Then, in the throes of yet another mentally abusive affair with a married

man, lethargy and unhappiness began to settle in. Psychotherapy was useful for revealing to Tess the underlying causes of her budding depression, but it seemed to have little curative effect on her symptoms. At this point, she made an appointment to see Dr. Peter Kramer, a psychiatrist in Rhode Island. Hoping to save her from the depression that had engulfed her mother, Dr. Kramer at first prescribed a drug called imipramine, the oldest of half a dozen or so antidepressants that doctors regularly relied upon. Tess improved as expected. "I am better," she told her doctor some weeks after beginning the drug therapy. "I am myself again."

But Tess was still mired in the hurtful affair that had in part prompted her first visit to Kramer, and she was having more trouble in her negotiations with a group of union leaders than she would have had before her depression. At about this time, the drug Prozac was approved by the U.S. Food and Drug Administration for use as an antidepressant. Dr. Kramer wrote out a prescription.

Within two weeks, Tess no longer reported a sense of weariness and depression—a feeling, she now saw, she had experienced and accepted as normal all her life. Her laugh became more genuine. She began to date other men and ended the relationship that had caused her such misery. She made new friends as she discovered that her old ones could only relate to her vanished depression. At work she gained a new self-confidence that enabled her to deal dispassionately with union demands and other issues.

Then, after several months in which Tess showed no symptoms of depression, Dr. Kramer began to wean her from Prozac, in accordance with the accepted practice for treating depression with medication. For a while, life went well for Tess, but by the time she had been off the drug for eight months, matters had deteriorated. The depression had not returned, but her zing was fading. "I'm not myself," she told her doctor, who put her back on the drug. "Who was I," wrote Kramer in *Listening to Prozac*, a book about the medication, "to withhold from her the bounties of science?" Tess, said the doctor, had undergone "a redefinition of self." What she once had accepted as her normal personality—not the depression so much as the low energy and unhappy relationships with men—now seemed alien.

The power of this chemical to alter the basic settings of personality raises a host of disturbing issues. Some psychiatrists question the wisdom of prescribing drugs that go well beyond the traditional restorative role for medicines. Just as anabolic steroids have been abused by athletes looking for a competitive edge, a "personality-in-a-pill" might be equally susceptible to abuse in an increasingly competitive society.

Of course, the very notion of changing one's personality at will calls into question the entire basis of self and identity. As Dr. Kramer wrote in reviewing his experience with Tess: "Charisma, courage, character, social competency—Prozac seemed to say that these and other concepts need to be reexamined, that our sense of what is constant in the self and what is mutable needs to be revised." Who is Scrooge, after all?

TOWARD A NEW SELF: THERAPY'S HORIZONS

Spurred by a desire—or at times an aching need—to change themselves, many people seek help to open the window on new possibilities in their personalities. Often, they turn to psychotherapists, the best of whom combine years of practical experience and research with a healthy measure of intuitive insight.

How—or why—therapy works is a very open question. The field includes as many as 400 different theories, giving rise to sometimes contradictory approaches to treatment. But most seem to achieve some degree of success for a wide range of disorders, perhaps because each approach addresses different facets of personality. The following pages describe a few of the major schools of therapy and how each might be applied to a different personality problem.

Given the variety of theories, most therapists practice eclecticism, tailoring a combination of techniques to each client. Some psychologists are even beginning to unite aspects of different schools into a single approach.

AIRING HIDDEN MOTIVES

Many therapists hold that psychological troubles stem from inner conflict caused by forces operating at an unconscious level. To bring this hidden discord to the surface, practitioners of so-called psychodynamic therapy tacitly encourage their clients to treat the therapist as the target of their emotional reactions—a technique known as transference—and to explore the network of unconscious associations by talking freely about problems.

The therapist tries to maintain an emotionally neutral, objective stance toward the client. This neutrality helps the client transfer old patterns of emotion from crucial relationships onto the relatively blank slate of the therapist, who, as a result, often becomes a replacement parent figure.

In treating someone with a dependent personality, for example, the therapist may point out that the client persistently asks the therapist for help with any decision, from going on a trip to doing his laundry. The client thus becomes aware that he is unconsciously behaving as if the therapist is a domineering parent. Increasing self-awareness leads to the realization that the client's feelings of dependence shape not only his attitude toward the therapist but his approach to other relationships as well.

Further exploration of the unconscious roots of his problems occurs when the client free-associates, talking about personal issues such as dreams or early childhood. In doing so, the client learns to abandon any inhibitions about revealing whatever comes to mind, a process that brings up symbols and connections that point to past events or repressed feelings. He may, for instance, associate a dream of helplessness at work with childhood memories of being criticized by his mother for some assertion of independence.

Sometimes, a sudden insight suffices to spark profound change. More often, though, the therapist must help the client to understand and confront these presumed unconscious forces.

LEARNING NEW PATTERNS

Another approach, known as cognitive behavior therapy, may appeal to those clients who believe that a direct focus on symptoms and a rational analysis of behavior are the keys to changing personality. Rather than assuming and looking for unconscious motivations, cognitive behavior therapy addresses personality problems by altering certain troublesome patterns of behavior and the misconceptions on which they are founded.

First, the therapist suggests that the client's problems stem from misguided beliefs that color the client's view of herself and her world, shaping her feelings and actions. In the case of an obsessive-compulsive perfectionist, for example, the underlying belief might be: "If I don't do everything perfectly, then I am worthless."

The therapist helps build a sense of collaboration by working with the client to draw up a list of problems. Together, they decide which should be dealt with first. The perfectionist might want to begin by, say, reducing interpersonal friction at work.

Then, to increase the client's awareness, the therapist may assign homework. For example, every night the client might record the day's dysfunctional thoughts and how she could have avoided them. (Some obsessive-compulsive people, however, can take this exercise too seriously, filling out extensive replies and counterreplies to their thoughts.) The client would also learn new ways to change her behavior—such as relaxation techniques to relieve anxiety.

These methods often help on a day-to-day basis, but the heart of cognitive behavior therapy involves changing the client's misguided notions. The therapist would thus assist her first to articulate her belief that perfection is the only worthy goal, then to understand how this attitude dominates her life. The final freedom from rigid, often repetitive routines comes when she manages to replace her perfectionist outlook with the more flexible and realistic view that she is a worthy person—even though she sometimes makes mistakes.

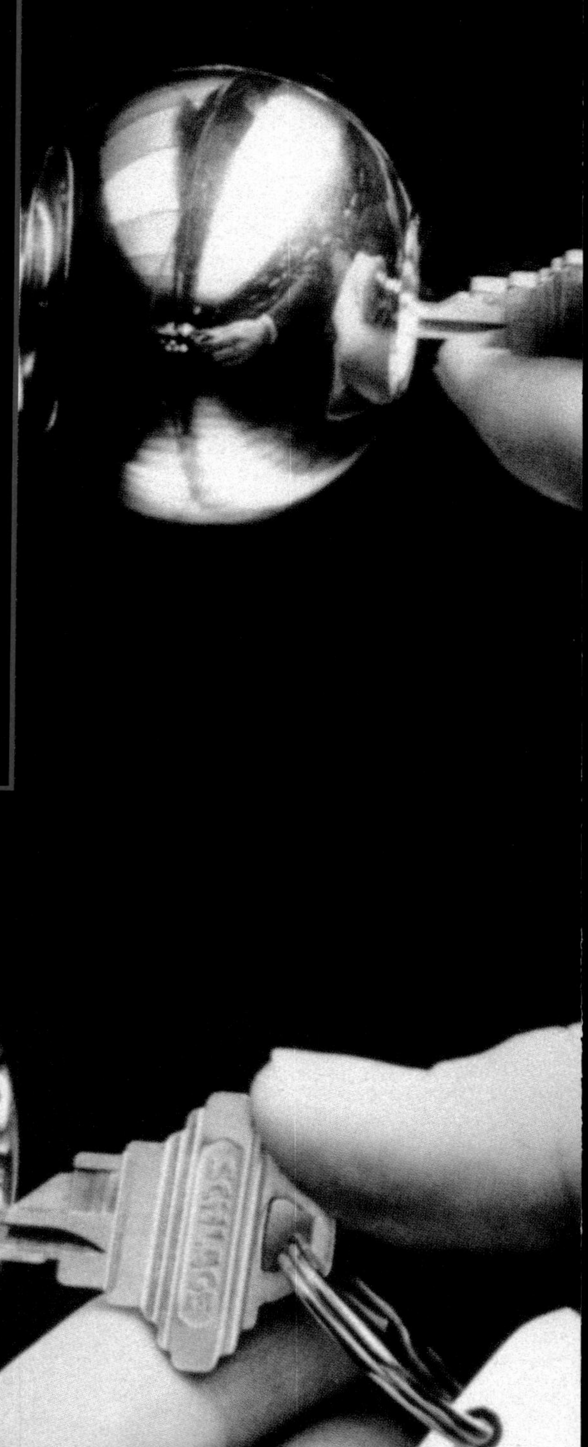

HEALING THE SOCIAL SELF

A third technique, called interpersonal therapy, looks at an individual's problems in the context of all his relationships—or his interpersonal field—rather than focusing on him as an isolated individual. In this instance, the therapist's main task is to help the client understand how he interacts with other people.

The therapist forms a diagnosis based on how the client relates to others in his daily life, not by deducing an elaborate inner psychic structure. For example, a client who tries to impress the therapist with overdramatized emotions and who complains about fleeting, unsatisfying relationships might be tentatively diagnosed as having a histrionic personality. But rather than probe for unconscious motives, the therapist would then ask the client about his most important relationships. A facile description of friends who adore and look after him, unable to resist his devastating charm, would help to confirm the therapist's initial supposition.

According to the interpersonal view, a child's personality develops in response to the parents' states of anxiety. As the child tries to prevent or soften these states by any means possible, patterns of interaction arise that the child will follow throughout his life. The therapist can explore these issues by asking the client about his role in his family.

The client's reliance on superficial qualities such as looks and his shallow but emotive ways of interacting with other people may well have stemmed from efforts to adapt to a troubled parent. He might have learned that he would be doted on and cared for if he stayed adorable and helpless, and he integrated this lesson into his very concept of himself.

After sessions of probing questions and thoughtful discussion, the client may come to realize that his dramatic appeal, though initially attractive, will not gain him the supportive relationships he seeks. By altering his view of himself and how he forms his relationships, he can learn new, more authentic ways of interacting with others.

THE GIFT OF EMPATHY

Some people seek in their therapist a surrogate friend, someone always ready to understand, support, and empathize. Although certain therapeutic techniques discourage this desire, so-called person-centered therapy suggests that such an approach can actually lead to lasting personality change, perhaps because it combines supportiveness with the attitude that the client is ultimately responsible for her own progress.

Person-centered therapy holds that the client has enormous potential for growth and change. The therapist encourages this potential by communicating empathy, and above all by showing unconditional support for the client, no matter what feelings or thoughts she reveals.

In this way, the therapist tries to establish a safe and secure relationship so that the client can willingly let negative thoughts emerge. The therapist echoes the client's concerns and helps to clarify them, but he does not impose his own interpretations.

Although this might seem to foster dependence on the therapist, the client actually directs her own therapy: She chooses what to discuss, evaluates how well the therapy is going, and ultimately decides when it should end. Conversely, the therapist does not diagnose or otherwise evaluate the client. For example, the client might come to her own realization that she subtly sabotages relationships by expressing anger indirectly. Unlike some other techniques, the therapist does not press for more information or try to label her condition but lets the client return to that theme when she chooses. In her own time, the theory goes, the client will be ready for further insights.

Under these conditions, the client learns to accept herself and to trust her own values. The therapist's emotional support has given her the confidence to confront aspects of herself that had been suppressed, and to gain faith not only in herself but also in her ability to change.

THE POWER OF THE GROUP

Theories of therapy differ, and so do the means of putting them into practice. A group approach, for instance, often helps in ways that one-on-one therapy cannot.

Although group members may come from different backgrounds and have quite different problems, the first few meetings tend to develop in the participants a strong sense of working together toward a common goal. Indeed, this attitude may be the most powerful healing aspect of group therapy. As trust builds, the individuals begin to share their emotions more openly—often changing the patterns of a lifetime to do so. At the same time, other members of the group learn from helping someone else through a painful experience.

Peer pressure, usually condemned in other contexts, has a positive effect here. In group therapy, members often are simply not allowed to get away with self-indulgent or destructive behavior. For example, a narcissistic group member might find that only anger or indifference greet him when he spouts off about himself. Meanwhile, the submissive members of the group learn to assert themselves better after dealing with the narcissist. Through a continuing process of such interactions, group members assist each other's healing—and find new opportunities for healing themselves.

GLOSSARY

Agoraphobia: a strong fear of being in public places or open areas, sometimes accompanied by panic attacks.
Antisocial disorder: a personality disorder marked by irresponsible behavior, lack of respect for law and custom, and the absence of remorse for harmful actions.
Anxiety: mental distress caused by the anticipation of threat or danger.
Avoidant disorder: a personality disorder marked by timidity, discomfort in social situations, and fear of rejection.
Behaviorism: the school of thought that psychology is the study of observable, quantifiable behavior.
Borderline disorder: a personality disorder marked by a pattern of instability in relationships, emotion, and self-image.
Compulsion: an irresistible urge to perform a repetitive or ritualistic act, especially one that is irrational.
Conditioned response: a response to an originally neutral stimulus acquired by the association of that stimulus with one naturally eliciting the response. By associating the sound of a bell with food, Pavlov created a conditioned response of salivation in dogs.
Dependent disorder: a personality disorder marked by submissive behavior and an inappropriate reliance on others.
Depression: a mood characterized by sadness, withdrawal, and negative thoughts. Extreme, or clinical, depression often requires treatment with drugs and psychotherapy.
Developmental psychology: a branch of psychology that studies changes in behavior as a function of growth throughout life.
Dopamine: a neurotransmitter involved in the regulation of emotion and movement.
Ego: in Freudian psychology, the part of the personality that governs interactions with the outside world. The ego mediates between biological drives and the environment. *See also* Id; Superego.
Enneagram: a geometric figure that diagrams nine basic human personality types and their relationships to one another.
Extraversion: part of the introversion-extraversion dimension of personality first identified by Carl Jung. An extravert's basic psychological orientation is toward the outside world of objects and people.
Five Factor Model: a model used by some trait psychologists that considers personality in terms of five groups of related traits, known as factors or personality domains.
Free association: in psychoanalysis, the uncensored reporting by the patient of thoughts, ideas, dreams, feelings, etc.
Gene: the basic unit of heredity, a length of DNA that codes for the production of a specific protein. Some theorists hold that aspects of personality are genetically based.
Hierarchy of needs: a classification system proposed by psychologist Abraham Maslow in which human needs and motives are ranked from the most basic, such as food, to the loftiest, such as the desire for justice.
Histrionic disorder: a personality disorder marked by excessive emotionality and attention seeking.
Humanist psychology: an approach to psychology that focuses on the uniqueness of human beings and takes into consideration human values and subjective experience.
Hysteria: an outdated term for a disorder marked by emotional outbursts and sensory and motor disturbances.
Id: in Freudian psychology, the part of the personality that consists of biological drives and instincts. *See also* Ego; Superego.
Introversion: part of the introversion-extraversion dimension of personality first identified by Carl Jung. An introvert's basic psychological orientation is inward, to the world of thoughts and concepts.
Multiple personality disorder (MPD): a rare disorder in which a person exhibits two or more well-developed personalities, each with characteristic behaviors and attitudes.
Myers-Briggs Type Indicator (MBTI): a psychological test that determines one of 16 personality types.
Narcissistic disorder: a personality disorder marked by a sense of self-importance and entitlement.
NEO personality inventory: a psychological test that measures personality in terms of five sets of traits. *See also* Five Factor Model.
Neurotransmitter: a chemical, synthesized by neurons, that carries information across the synapse from one neuron to another.
Obsessive-compulsive personality disorder: a personality disorder marked by inflexibility and perfectionism.
Paranoid disorder: a personality disorder marked by an undue mistrust of other people.
Passive-aggressive disorder: a personality disorder marked by resistance to the demands of others through indirect and passive behavior such as procrastination.
Personality disorder: any of several conditions involving rigid personality traits that limit adaptability and often cause social and professional difficulties. *See also specific disorders.*
Phobia: an irrational fear of an activity, situation, or object.

Psychoanalysis: originated by Sigmund Freud, a theory of personality that emphasizes the role of repressed thoughts and emotions; also a technique of psychotherapy that attempts to bring repressed thoughts and emotions to the surface.
Psychotherapy: the treatment of psychological problems through psychological means, usually with any of several techniques such as psychoanalysis or humanist therapy.
Reinforcement: a procedure that uses either rewards or punishments in order to alter a response.
Schizoid disorder: a personality disorder marked by withdrawal and emotional indifference.
Schizophrenia: a group of severe mental disorders characterized by such symptoms as disorganized thought, speech, movement, and behavior; flat emotions; delusions; and general withdrawal from family, society, and reality.
Schizotypal disorder: a personality disorder, marked by peculiar thinking and behavior, that resembles schizophrenia but is not as severe.
Self-actualization: in humanist psychology, the full realization of one's potential.
Serotonin: a neurotransmitter involved in mood disorders such as depression, as well as in the regulation of temperature and sleep.
Superego: in Freudian psychology, the part of the mind that internalizes the influences, values, and standards of parents and culture. *See also* Ego; Id.
Talking therapy: psychotherapy that involves such techniques as free association and that does not include medication.
Trait: an enduring pattern of perception, thought, or behavior in an individual.
Trait psychology: the psychological theory that personality can best be studied in terms of a set of stable characteristics.

BIBLIOGRAPHY

BOOKS

Allport, Gordon W. *Personality: A Psychological Interpretation*. New York: Henry Holt, 1937.

Appel, Willa. *Cults in America: Programmed for Paradise*. New York: Holt, Rinehart and Winston, 1983.

Aronson, Morton J., and Melvin A. Scharfman (editors). *Psychotherapy: The Analytic Approach*. Northvale, New Jersey: Jason Aronson, 1992.

Barnouw, Victor. *Culture and Personality* (4th edition). Homewood, Illinois: Dorsey Press, 1985.

Bates, Daniel G., and Fred Plog. *Cultural Anthropology* (3d edition). New York: McGraw-Hill, 1980.

Bear, David, Roy Freeman, and Mark Greenberg. "Changes in Personality Associated with Neurologic Disease." In *Psychiatry*, edited by Jesse O. Cavenar. Philadelphia: J. B. Lippincott, 1985.

Beck, Aaron T., Arthur Freeman, and Associates. *Cognitive Therapy of Personality Disorders*. New York: Guilford Press, 1990.

Bellak, Leopold. *The Thematic Apperception Test, the Children's Apperception Test, and the Senior Apperception Technique in Clinical Use* (5th edition). Boston, Massachusetts: Allyn and Bacon, 1993.

Benjamin, Lorna Smith. *Interpersonal Diagnosis and Treatment of Personality Disorders*. New York: Guilford Press, 1993.

Bloom, Floyd E., and Arlyne Lazerson. *Brain, Mind, and Behavior* (2d edition). New York: W. H. Freeman, 1988.

Bock, Philip K. *Rethinking Psychological Anthropology: Continuity and Change in the Study of Human Action*. New York: W. H. Freeman, 1988.

Brody, Nathan. *Personality: In Search of Individuality*. New York: Academic Press, 1988.

Burstein, Alvin G., and Sandra Loucks. *Rorschach's Test: Scoring and Interpretation*. New York: Hemisphere, 1989.

Carver, Charles S., and Michael F. Scheier. *Perspectives on Personality*. Boston, Massachusetts: Allyn and Bacon, 1988.

Castle, Kit, and Stefan Bechtel. *Katherine, It's Time*. New York: Harper and Row, 1989.

Colson, Charles W. *Loving God*. Grand Rapids, Michigan: Zondervan, 1983.

Corsini, Raymond J., and Danny Wedding. *Current Psychotherapies* (4th edition). Itasca, Illinois: F. E. Peacock, 1989.

Crompton, Paul. *The T'ai Chi Workbook*. Boston, Massachusetts: Shambhala, 1987.

Davidson, Shamai. *Holding on to Humanity—The Message of Holocaust Survivors: The Shamai Davidson Papers*. New York: New York University Press, 1992.

Diagnostic and Statistical Manual of Mental Disorders (3d edition). Washington, D.C.: American Psychiatric Association, 1987.

Diamant, Louis (editor). *Psychology of Sports, Exercise, and Fitness*. New York: Hemisphere, 1991.

Diamond, Solomon (editor). *The Roots of Psychology*. New York: Basic Books, 1974.

Dicks, Shirley. *From Vietnam to Hell: Interviews with Victims of Post-Traumatic Stress Disorder*. Jefferson, North Carolina: McFarland, 1990.

Exner, John E., Jr. *A Rorschach Workbook for the Comprehensive System* (3d edition). Asheville, North Carolina: Rorschach Workshops, 1990.

Eysenck, Hans J.:
Decline and Fall of the Freudian Empire. Washington, D.C.: Scott-Townsend Publishers, 1990.
Psychology Is about People. New York: Library Press, 1972.

Feldman, Robert S., and Linda F. Quenzer. *Fundamentals of Neuropsychopharmacology*. Sunderland, Massachusetts: Sinauer Associates, 1984.

Freedheim, Donald K. (editor). *History of Psychotherapy: A Century of Change*. Washington, D.C.: American Psychological Association, 1992.

Freeman, Arthur, et al. *Clinical Applications of Cognitive Therapy*. New York: Plenum Press, 1990.

Freeman, Arthur, et al. (editors). *Comprehensive Handbook of Cognitive Therapy*. New York: Plenum Press, 1989.

Freeman, Arthur, and Frank M. Dattilio (editors). *Comprehensive Casebook of Cognitive Therapy*. New York: Plenum Press, 1992.

Freeman, Eileen Elias. *Touched by Angels*. New York: Warner Books, 1993.

Galanter, Marc. *Cults: Faith, Healing, and Coercion*. New York: Oxford University Press, 1989.

Glassman, Ronald M., and William H. Swatos Jr. (editors). *Charisma, History, and Social Structure*. Westport, Connecticut: Greenwood Press, 1986.

Hall, Calvin S., and Vernon J. Nordby. *A Primer of Jungian Psychology*. New York: Mentor, 1973.

Hartmann, Ernest. *Boundaries in the Mind*. New York: Basic Books, 1991.

Hassan, Steve. *Combatting Cult Mind Control*. Rochester, Vermont: Park Street Press, 1988.

Helmreich, William B. *Against All Odds*. New York: Simon and Schuster, 1992.

A History of Psychology in Autobiography. Worcester, Massachusetts: Clark University Press, 1936.

Horn, A. S., J. Korf, and B. H. C. Westerink (editors). *The Neurobiology of Dopamine*. New York: Academic Press, 1979.

Horowitz, Mardi Jon. *Stress Response Syndromes* (2d edition). Northvale, New Jersey: Jason Aronson, 1986.

Hunt, Morton. *The Story of Psychology*. New York: Doubleday, 1993.

James, William. *The Varieties of Religious Experience*. New York: Penguin Books, 1982.

Jenike, Michael A., and Marie Åsberg (editors). *Understanding Obsessive-Compulsive Disorder* (OCD). Toronto: Hogrefe and Huber, 1991.

Jenike, Michael A., Lee Baer, and William E. Minichiello. *Obsessive-Compulsive Disorders: Theory and Management*. Chicago: Year Book Medical Publishers, 1990.

Johnson, Sheila K. *The Japanese through American Eyes*. Stanford, California: Stanford University Press, 1988.

Jung, Carl G. *Psychological Types*. Princeton, New Jersey: Princeton University Press, 1971.

Kahn, Samuel. *T.A.T. and Understanding People*. New York: Vantage Press, 1966.

Kamala, Srimati. *Mahatma Gandhi: An American Profile*. New Delhi, India: The Gandhi Peace Foundation, 1987.

Kantor, Martin. *Diagnosis and Treatment of the Personality Disorders*. St. Louis, Missouri: Ishiyaku EuroAmerica, 1992.

Kaplan, Harold I., and Benjamin J. Sadock. *Synopsis of Psychiatry* (6th edition). Baltimore, Maryland: Williams and Wilkins, 1991.

Kaplan, Harold I., and Benjamin J. Sadock (editors). *Comprehensive Group Psychotherapy* (2d edition). Baltimore, Maryland: Williams and Wilkins, 1983.

Keirsey, David, and Marilyn Bates. *Please Understand Me: Character and Temperament Types* (5th edition). Del Mar, California: Gnosology Books, 1984.

Kirschenbaum, Howard, and Valerie Land Henderson (editors). *The Carl Rogers Reader*. Boston, Massachusetts: Houghton Mifflin, 1989.

Kluft, Estelle S. "A Literary Overview of Multiple Personality Disorder." In *Expressive and Functional Therapies in the Treatment of Multiple Personality Disorder*, edited by Estelle S. Kluft. Springfield, Illinois: Charles C. Thomas, 1993.

Kramer, Peter D. *Listening to Prozac*. New York: Viking, 1993.

Kutash, Irwin L., and Alexander Wolf (editors). *Psychotherapist's Casebook*. San Francisco: Jossey-Bass, 1986.

Lawry, John D. *Guide to the History of Psychology*. Totowa, New Jersey: Littlefield, Adams, 1981.

Levinson, Daniel J., et al. *The Seasons of a Man's Life*. New York: Ballantine Books, 1978.

Lietaer, G., J. Rombauts, and R. Van Balen (editors). *Client-Centered and Experiential Psychotherapy in the Nineties*. Louvain, Belgium: Leuven University Press, 1990.

Lindholm, Charles. *Charisma*. Cambridge,

Massachusetts: Basil Blackwell, 1990.

Lowenthal, Wolfe. *There Are No Secrets.* Berkeley, California: North Atlantic Books, 1991.

McCrae, Robert R., and Paul T. Costa Jr. *Personality in Adulthood.* New York: Guilford Press, 1990.

Madsen, Douglas, and Peter G. Snow. *The Charismatic Bond: Political Behavior in Time of Crisis.* Cambridge, Massachusetts: Harvard University Press, 1991.

Melville, Joy. *Phobias and Obsessions.* London: George Allen and Unwin, 1977.

Meyer, Jeffrey F. "The Right Place is Here, the Right Time is Now: Taiji as Mental and Physical Therapy." In *Psychology of Sports, Exercise, and Fitness,* edited by Louis Diamant. New York: Hemisphere, 1991.

Meyer, Robert G. *The Clinician's Handbook: Integrated Diagnostics, Assessment, and Intervention in Adult and Adolescent Psychopathology* (3d edition). Boston, Massachusetts: Allyn and Bacon, 1993.

Monte, Christopher F. *Beneath the Mask* (4th edition). Fort Worth, Texas: Harcourt Brace Jovanovich College Publishers, 1991.

Myers, Isabel Briggs, and Peter B. Myers. *Gifts Differing.* Palo Alto, California: Consulting Psychologists Press, 1980.

Norcross, John C., and Marvin R. Goldfried (editors). *Handbook of Psychotherapy Integration.* New York: Basic Books, 1992.

Patrick, Ted. *Let Our Children Go!* New York: E. P. Dutton, 1976.

Pervin, Lawrence A. *Personality: Theory and Research* (5th edition).New York: John Wiley and Sons, 1989.

Psychophysiology: Systems, Processes, and Applications. New York: Guilford Press, 1986.

Putnam, Frank W. *Diagnosis and Treatment of Multiple Personality Disorder.* New York: Guilford Press, 1989.

Raine, Adrian. *The Psychopathology of Crime: Criminal Behavior as a Clinical Disorder.* San Diego: Academic Press, in press.

Restak, Richard M. *The Brain.* New York: Bantam Books, 1984.

Ring, Kenneth. *Heading Toward Omega.* New York: William Morrow, 1984.

Riso, Don Richard:

Discovering Your Personality Type: The Enneagram Questionnaire. Boston, Massachusetts: Houghton Mifflin, 1992.

Personality Types: Using the Enneagram for Self-Discovery. Boston, Massachusetts: Houghton Mifflin, 1987.

Ross, Colin A. *Multiple Personality Disorder: Diagnosis, Clinical Features, and Treatment.* New York: John Wiley and Sons, 1989.

Schwartz, Theodore, Geoffrey M. White, and Catherine A. Lutz (editors). *New Directions in Psychological Anthropology.* New York: Cambridge University Press, 1992.

Sheehy, Gail. *Passages.* New York: Bantam Books, 1976.

Shweder, Richard A. *Thinking through Cultures.* Cambridge, Massachusetts: Harvard University Press, 1991.

Siever, Larry J., and Kenneth S. Kendler. "Schizoid/Schizotypal/Paranoid Personality Disorders." In *Psychiatry.* Philadelphia: J. B. Lippincott, 1985.

Stigler, James W., Richard A. Shweder, and Gilbert Herdt. *Cultural Psychology: Essays on Comparative Human Development.* New York: Cambridge University Press, 1990.

Suarez-Orozco, Marcelo M. *Central American Refugees and U.S. High Schools.* Stanford, California: Stanford University Press, 1989.

Van der Kolk, Bessel A. "The Psychological Consequences of Overwhelming Life Experiences." In *Psychological Trauma,* edited by Bessel A. van der Kolk. Washington, D.C.: American Psychiatric Press, 1987.

Wilkerson, David. *The Cross and the Switchblade.* New York: Jove Books, 1962.

Willner, Ann Ruth. *The Spellbinders: Charismatic Political Leadership.* New Haven, Connecticut: Yale University Press, 1984.

Yalom, Irvin D. *The Theory and Practice of Group Psychotherapy* (3d edition). New York: Basic Books, 1985.

PERIODICALS

Angelo, Bonnie. "Life at the End of the Rainbow." *Time,* November 4, 1991.

Barlam, Cathy. "Women on the Verge: The Surge in Borderline Personality Disorder." *Mademoiselle,* November 1989.

Barnes, Deborah M. "Biological Issues in Schizophrenia." *Science,* January 23, 1987.

Bellafante, Ginia. "Taking the Bungee Plunge." *Utne Reader,* May/June 1992.

Bensimhon, Dan. "Take Some Risks Now and Then. The Doctor Says It Will Be Good For You." *Men's Health,* April 1992.

Braun, Bennett G.:

"Neurophysiologic Changes in Multiple Personality Due to Integration: A Preliminary Report." *American Journal of Clinical Hypnosis,* October 1983.

"Psychophysiologic Phenomena in Multiple Personality and Hypnosis." *American Journal of Clinical Hypnosis,* October 1983.

Chance, Paul:

"The Divided Self." *Psychology Today,* September 1986.

"Free Spirits." *Psychology Today,* April 1989.

Cohen, Barry M., and Carol T. Cox. "Breaking the Code: Identification of Multiplicity through Art Productions." *Treating Abuse Today,* May/June 1991.

Collett, Lily. "Step by Step." *Mother Jones,*

July/August 1988.

"Deprogrammers to the Rescue: Some Call It Kidnapping." *Congressional Quarterly*, May 7, 1993.

Dobkin, Bruce. "A Torrid Affair." *Discover*, June 1992.

Fernald, Anne, and Hiromi Morikawa. "Common Themes and Cultural Variations in Japanese and American Mothers' Speech to Infants." *Child Development*, June 1993.

Finkenberg, Mel E. "Effect of Participation in Taekwondo on College Women's Self-Concept." *Perceptual and Motor Skills*, 1990.

Freeman, Philip S., and John G. Gunderson. "Treatment of Personality Disorders." *Psychiatric Annals*, March 1989.

Gallagher, Winifred. "The Torment of Multiple-Personality Disorder." *Cosmopolitan*, November 1990.

Gibbs, Nancy. "Fire Storm in Waco." *Time*, May 3, 1993.

Goleman, Daniel. "Your Unconscious Mind May Be Smarter Than You." *New York Times*, June 23, 1992.

Goode, Erica E. "Psychic Borderlines." *U.S. News and World Report*, January 20, 1992.

Goode, Erica E., and Betsy Wagner. "Does Psychotherapy Work?" *U.S. News and World Report*, May 24, 1993.

Greyson, Bruce. "Near-Death Experiences and Personal Values." *American Journal of Psychiatry*, May 1983.

Herbert, W. "The Three Brains of Eve: EEG Data." *Science News*, May 29, 1982.

Higdon, John F. "Expressive Therapy in Conjunction with Psychotherapy in the Treatment of Persons with Multiple Personality Disorder." *American Journal of Occupational Therapy*, November 1990.

Hollan, Douglas. "Cross-Cultural Differences in the Self." *Journal of Anthropological Research*, Winter 1992.

Horgan, John. "Eugenics Revisited." *Scientific American*, June 1993.

Hubbard, Kim. "Exploring a Last Taboo." *People*, June 1, 1992.

Hughes, John R., et al. "Brain Mapping in a Case of Multiple Personality." *Clinical Electroencephalography*, 1990, Vol. 21, No. 4.

Hunt, Morton. "Blue Skies Ahead." *American Health*, October 1991.

Iyer, Pico. "Of Weirdos and Eccentrics." *Time*, January 18, 1988.

Jacoby, Susan. "Me, Myself, and I: Those Needy, Needy Narcissists." *Cosmopolitan*, September 1992.

"Jonestown, Guyana Cult Deaths Raised to 911; Bodies Removed by U.S. Troops, Flown to Delaware Air Base." *Facts on File Yearbook*, December 1, 1978.

Kevles, Daniel J. "Controlling the Genetic Arsenal." *Wilson Quarterly*, Spring 1992.

Lacayo, Richard:
"Cult of Death." *Time*, March 15, 1993.
"In the Grip of a Psychopath." *Time*, May 3, 1993.

Landers, Peggy. "The Eight Lives of Juanita." *Miami Herald*, August 5, 1990.

"Life After the Lottery." *Fortune*, September 3, 1984.

Loewenstein, Richard J. (editor). *The Psychiatric Clinics of North America: Multiple Personality Disorder*, September 1991.

Lubenow, Gerald C. "A Passion for Potatoes." *Newsweek*, May 30, 1988.

Lynn, Steven Jay, and Judith W. Rhue. "Fantasy Proneness: Hypnosis, Developmental Antecedents, and Psychopathology." *American Psychologist*, January 1988.

Marin, Deborah B., et al. "Biological Models and Treatments for Personality Disorders." *Psychiatric Annals*, March 1989.

Markus, Hazel Rose, and Shinobu Kitayama. "Culture and the Self: Implications for Cognition, Emotion, and Motivation." *Psychological Review*, April 1991.

Mathew, R. J. "Personality of Regional Cerebral Bloodflow." *British Journal of Psychiatry*, May 1984.

Maxwell, Jessica. "Fantasia." *Omni*, June 1988.

Mauro, James. "Bright Lights, Big Mystery." *Psychology Today*, July/August 1992.

Mesic, Penelope. "Presence of Minds." *Chicago*, September 1992.

"The Messiah of Waco." *Newsweek*, March 15, 1993.

Miller, D. Patrick. "What's Your Number?" *Yoga Journal*, January/February 1993.

Miller, Scott D., and Patrick Triggiano. "The Psychophysiological Investigation of Multiple Personality Disorder: Review and Update." *American Journal of Clinical Hypnosis*, July 1992.

Norcross, John C., Diane J. Strausser, and Frank J. Faltus. "The Therapist's Therapist." *American Journal of Psychotherapy*, January 1988.

Ogden, Christopher. "Rise of the American Oddball." *Time*, June 6, 1988.

Orth, Maureen. "Blueblood War." *Vanity Fair*, April 1993.

Petrow, Jay. "Ankles Aweigh: Notes from a Bungee Jumper." *Business Week*, July 13, 1992.

"Psychic Borderlines." *U.S. News and World Report*, January 20, 1992.

Putnam, Frank W. "Altered States: Peeling Away the Layers of a Multiple Personality." *The Sciences*, November/December 1992.

Rainie, Harrison. "The Final Days of David Koresh." *U.S. News and World Report*, May 3, 1993.

Rapoport, Judith L. "The Biology of Obsessions and Compulsions." *Scientific Ameri-*

can, March 1989.

Restak, Richard M. "See No Evil." *The Sciences*, July/August 1992.

Rieff, David. "Victims, All?" *Harper's Magazine*, October 1991.

Rosenthal, Doreen A., and S. Shirley Feldman. "The Acculturation of Chinese Immigrants: Perceived Effects on Family Functioning of Length of Residence in Two Cultural Contexts." *Journal of Genetic Psychology*, 1990, Vol. 151, No. 4.

Seligmann, Jean. "Menopause." *Newsweek*, May 25, 1992.

Sell, Charles M. "Sins of the Fathers (and Mothers)." *Christianity Today*, September 10, 1990.

"Serotonin: Neurotransmitter of the '90s." *Psychology Today*, September/October 1992.

Shweder, Richard A., and Maria A. Sullivan. "Cultural Psychology: Who Needs It?" *Annual Review of Psychology*, 1993.

Siever, Larry J., and Kenneth L. Davis. "A Psychobiological Perspective on the Personality Disorders." *American Journal of Psychiatry*, December 1991.

"Spiritus contra Spiritum: The Bill Wilson/C. G. Jung Letters." *Parabola*, Summer 1987.

"U.S. Congressman, Four Others Killed in Guyana Ambush; Hundreds Commit Suicide at American Religious Commune." *Facts on File Yearbook*, November 24, 1978.

Wallis, Claudia, and James Willwerth. "Schizophrenia: A New Drug Brings Patients Back to Life." *Time*, July 6, 1992.

Widiger, Thomas A. "Prevalence and Comorbidity of Personality Disorders." *Psychiatric Annals*, March 1989.

Wittkowski, Michael. "No Longer the Biggest Lottery Winner Ever, A Chicagoan Reclaims A Different Prize: His Privacy." *People*, November 22, 1987.

OTHER SOURCES

Block, Jack. "A Contrarian View of the Five-Factor Approach to Personality Description." Berkeley, California: University of California, 1993.

Haidt, Jonathan, Silvia Helena Koller, and Maria G. Dias. "Affect, Culture, and the Morality of Harmless Offenses." Chicago, Illinois: Committee on Human Development, University of Chicago, March 13, 1993.

"Multiple Personalities: The Search for Deadly Memories." HBO documentary videotape, 1993.

"Parents Teach Babies Cultures in Unique Ways." Morning Edition, Segment #16. Washington, D.C.: National Public Radio, July 15, 1993.

Pelikan, Helen L. "Psychological Type, MBTI, and Culture." Interview with Katharine D. Myers and Gary R. Weaver. Bethesda, Maryland: Pelikan Associates, August 25, 1992.

Riso, Don Richard. "Enneagram Personality Types." Brochure discussing the Enneagram method. New York: Enneagram Personality Types, 1992.

INDEX

Page numbers in boldface refer to illustrations or illustrated text.

A

B

C

D

E

Q

R

S

PICTURE CREDITS

The sources for the illustrations for this book are listed below. Credits from left to right are separated by semicolons; credits from top to bottom by dashes.

Cover: Evan H. Sheppard. **7:** © Paul Elledge, MT/Panoramic Images, Chicago 1993—Barbara Campbell/Gamma-Liaison—Don Bonsey/Tony Stone Images—Jim Arndt Photography, inset Charlotte Mowrey, hand tinting by Jim Littles. **8, 9:** Background Geoffrey Gove/Image Bank, Archives of the History of American Psychology; Mary Evans Picture Library, London/Sigmund Freud Copyrights; Archives of the History of American Psychology, image manipulation by Time-Life Books. **13:** Rorschach, H., *Psychodiagnostics*, Plates, ©1921 Verlag Hans Huber, Bern (renewed 1948). **14:** Mary Evans Picture Library, London/Sigmund Freud Copyrights. **15:** National Library of Medicine. **16:** *Cumulative Record: A Selection of Papers*, 3d edition, p. 143, reprinted with permission from the B. F. Skinner Foundation. **18, 19:** Art by John Drummond. **21:** Reprinted from *Thematic Apperception Test*, Harvard University Press, ©1943 the President and Fellows of Harvard College, ©1971 Henry A. Murray. **23:** Mary Evans Picture Library, London/Sigmund Freud Copyrights, courtesy W. E. Freud; Archives of the History of American Psychology. **24:** Courtesy Andreas Jung; Archives of the History of American Psychology. **25:** Archives of the History of American Psychology, except center H. J. Eysenck, London. **27:** Tony Stone Images. **28:** © Paul Elledge, MT/Panoramic Images, Chicago 1993. **29:** Chart by Fatima Taylor. **30:** Christopher Bissell/Tony Stone Images. **31:** Modified and reproduced by special permission of the Publisher, Consulting Psychologists Press, Inc., Palo Alto, Calif. 94303 from *Introduction to Type*® by Isabel Briggs Myers. Revised by Linda K. Kirby and Katharine D. Myers.©1993 Consulting Psychologists

Press, Inc. All rights reserved. Further reproduction is prohibited without the Publisher's written consent. **32:** Bruce Ayers/Tony Stone Images. **33:** Reproduced by special permission of the Publisher, Psychological Assessment Resources, Inc., 16204 North Florida Avenue, Lutz, Fla. 33549, from the NEO *Personality Inventory, Revised*, by Paul Costa and Robert McCrae, ©1978, 1985, 1989, 1992 PAR, Inc. Further reproduction is prohibited without permission of PAR, Inc. **34, 35:** P. Motta/SPL/Photo Researchers. **36, 37:** David York/The Stock Shop, Medichrome; Erika Stone/Photo Researchers; P. Motta/SPL/Photo Researchers. **38, 39:** Daniel McDonald/The Stock Shop, Medichrome; Jose Luis Pelaez; art by Stephen R. Wagner; Dr. Georg Stenberg, University of Lund, Sweden. **40, 41:** R. Landau/Westlight; art by Stephen R. Wagner. **42, 43:** Barbara Campbell/Gamma-Liaison. **45:** Harlow Primate Laboratory, University of Wisconsin. **47:** Terry Vine/Tony Stone Images. **48:** Hideo Ozawa/Photonica. **50:** Frilet/Sipa Press; ©Tony O'Brien. **52:** Jay Shurley. **54, 55:** Lawrence Manning/Black Star; art by Alfred T. Kamajian. **56-63:** Background art by Alfred T. Kamajian. **56, 57:** Fred Ward/Black Star, image manipulation by Time-Life Books. **58:** Courtesy Bambi B. Schieffelin, image manipulation by Time-Life Books. **60:** John F. Conn, image manipulation by Time-Life Books. **62:** Adina Tovy/The Stock Shop, image manipulation by Time-Life Books. **65:** NASA. **68, 69:** Photo by Evan H. Sheppard, photo illustration by Stephen R. Wagner. **71:** Art by Stephen R. Wagner. **72:** Paul Chesley—National Portrait Gallery, London. **75:** Breiter and Cohen/*Science*, July 30, 1993, p. 556. **79:** © L. Manning/Westlight, except center; Adrian Raine. **80:** The Miami Herald/ David Walters. **82:** The Ministry of Information and Broadcasting, Government of India; Roger-Viollet, Paris. **83:** Gamma-Liaison. **85:** David Hume Kennerly/*Time Magazine*; Greg Robinson, San Francisco Examiner/UPI. **88, 89:** Stuart Franklin/Magnum. **90, 91:** Hakan Ludwigsson. **93:** Photo and image manipulation by Fil Hunter. **94, 95:** Courtesy Kit Castle/from *Katherine, It's Time*, Harper and Row, New York, 1989. **96, 97:** Don Bonsey/Tony Stone Images—Dr. Bennett G. Braun, M.D./Associate Mental Health Services. **98, 99:** Background photo and image manipulation by Fil Hunter, artwork courtesy Barry M. Cohen, Psychiatric Institute of Washington, D.C. **100, 101:** David Teplica M.D., M.F.A., courtesy The Collected Image, Evanston, Ill. **103:** K. Martin-Kuri, *Angel of the Blue Dawn*, ©1987, Tapestry, P.O. Box 3032, Waquoit, Mass. 02536, 1-800-28ANGEL. **106, 107:** Lynn Johnson/Black Star—*Archives of General Psychiatry*, ©1992, American Medical Association, September 1992, Vol. 49, p. 685. **109:** *People Weekly*, ©1987 Manny Crisostomo. **111:** David Modell, London. **114:** Comstock, Inc.—Comstock, Inc./Gary Benson—Comstock, Inc. (4). **115:** Modified and reproduced by special permission of the Publisher, Consulting Psychologists Press, Inc., Palo Alto, Calif. 94303 from *Introduction to Type*® by Isabel Briggs Myers. Revised by Linda K. Kirby and Katharine D. Myers. ©1993 Consulting Psychologists Press, Inc. All rights reserved. Further reproduction is prohibited without the Publisher's written consent. **119:** Wolfgang Volz/Bilderberg. **121:** Superstock, hand tinting by Jim Littles. **122, 123:** Jim Arndt Photography, inset Charlotte Mowrey, hand tinting by Jim Littles. **124, 125:** Jon Riley/Tony Stone Images, hand tinting by Jim Littles. **126, 127:** Jay Maisel Photography, hand tinting by Jim Littles. **128, 129:** Terry Vine/Tony Stone Images, hand tinting by Jim Littles. **130, 131:** Evan H. Sheppard, courtesy Morrison House, Alexandria, Va., hand tinting by Jim Littles.

ACKNOWLEDGMENTS

The editors of *The Enigma of Personality* would like to thank these individuals for their valuable contributions:

Kit Castle; Susan Curtiss, University of California, Los Angeles; Rif El-Mallakh, University of Louisville, Louisville, Ky.; Hans J. Eysenck, London; William Graziano, Texas A&M University, College Station, Tex.; Jonathan Haidt, University of Chicago, Chicago; Klaus D. Hoppe, University of California, Los Angeles; Mardi J. Horowitz, University of California, San Francisco; John Hughes, University of Illinois, Chicago; Declan Jarry, Morrison House, Alexandria, Va.; Peter Kramer, Brown University, Providence; Arthur Lecesse, Kenyon College, Gambier, Ohio; Roy J. Mathew, Duke University Medical Center, Durham, N.C.; Robert McCrae, Gerontology Research Center, Baltimore, Md.; Herbert Meltzer, Case Western Reserve University, Cleveland; Peggy Miller, University of Illinois, Urbana; Scott Miller, River Hills, Wis.; Julie Mossing, Associated Mental Health, Skokie, Ill.; Ruth Munroe, Pitzer College, Claremont, Calif.; Helen Pelikan, Pelikan Associates, Bethesda, Md.; Adrian Raine, University of Southern California, Los Angeles; R. J. Sanders, Alexandria, Va.; Bambi Schieffelin, New York University, New York; Jeffrey Schwartz, University of California, Los Angeles; Jay Shurley, Oklahoma City; R. Bob Smith III, Psychological Assessment Resources, Odessa, Fla.; Charles Stangor, University of Maryland, College Park; Marcelo Suarez-Orozco, University of California, San Diego; Steve West, Arizona State University, Tempe.